Dear Steve + Val,

Enjoy!

Barbara Kodet Mages

TO BECHYN
AND BACK

BARBARA KODET MAGES

DEDICATION

. . . .

I was asked to write a book about growing up near Bechyn, Minnesota, and I said, "I can't write a book." "At least write some of your stories," so I did, and they were printed in our monthly family newsletter called the, "Family Reunion." Now we are including these stories written about growing up on a farm in the, "Great Depression," and then, "World War II."

I want to dedicate this book to my family, especially to Linda who typed every word, trying to decipher my handwriting, and also printing the, "Family Reunion." To my daughter, Donna, who started the, "Family Reunion," almost nineteen years ago. To my son, Larry, who kept asking me to write. To my son, Rick who came up with the title, "To Bechyn and Back" To Gina Gall Andersen, my Granddaughter who organized the printing. Also to my sons and daughters who kept encouraging me, to my Grandchildren who have been reading my stories to their children, my dear Great Grandchildren.

1932, Barbara with her
Teddy Bear at three years old

BARBARA KODET MAGES

Barbara Kodet Mages lives in Sleepy Eye, Minnesota, just forty miles away from her childhood home near Bechyn, Minnesota. She and her husband, Alphonse, enjoyed many years together before he passed away in 2009, at the age of eighty-one, one day after their sixty- third wedding anniversary. The year is now 2015.

Together, they raised sixteen children, nine sons and seven daughters- Linda, (Joe) Gall, Daniel, (Arlene), Nancy, (Chuck) Strate, Larry, (Maggie), Duane, (Jermayne), Rick, (Jane), Barbara, (Kevin) Plath, Elizabeth Jass, John, (Cindy), Jeffrey, (LeAnn), Curtis, (Kathy), Debra, (Larry) Fischer, Donna, (Dean) Nelson, Thomas, (Sharon), Michael, (Amy), and Lisa, (Tony) Schmitz. They all live in Minnesota. She has many grandchildren and great grandchildren.

Barbara has three living sisters, and one brother, who get together often during the year, Martha, (Clarence) Serbus, Adella, (Albin) Mages, Mary Lou, (Jim) Butzer and Alois Jr. (Junior.) Her siblings have all lost their spouses, but they all live in their own homes. When Dad and Mother retired, and moved to Olivia, Minnesota, my brother, Alois Jr. took over, and lived there with his family. Now his son, Dan Kodet, and his family are keeping up the management of the Kodet Farm.

L-R: Front, Martha, Lydia, Mother, Dad, Mary Lou. L-R: Back, Ed, Emil, Barbara, Adella, Johanna, Alois Jr.

TABLE OF CONTENTS

CHAPTER ONE
School Days from the Past

· ·

One of my earliest memories is of my first day of school. Our one room school was District 12, little more than a mile and a half away from our farm, by Bechyn, Minnesota. I was five years old, and we walked to school. Because I was the, "little one," my brother, Ed and I were going to start out sooner, and my sisters, Lydia and Martha would come later. Ed was in the sixth grade, and we started walking east along the field road, then cut across the pasture until we got to the road. Ed said, "Let's trot." (now we say jog). So we trot all the way to school. Every day until it got real cold, or it rained, then my Dad would give us a ride in our 1931 Model A car. When the snow got deep in the winter, Dad would hook up the team of horses to a sleigh, and we'd cover up with blankets when he drove us to school. There were no snowplows to clean the roads. In the spring the men would get together, and shovel off the snow banks.

We had one teacher, Celia Kodet, for our school of over 20 children in all eight grades. I had three other classmates in the first grade. She was my teacher for four years. I went to this country school for eight years. Each spring we had a, "Play Day," with other schools. There were prizes for the winning teams in softball and, other races. Also art was displayed, and songs were sung.

Each Christmas season a stage was built, and curtains hung on the west end of the school. The public was invited to a

Christmas program with Carols being sung, and poems by the younger children, and skits and plays put on by the older children. Santa would come after the program, gifts were exchanged, and lunch was served to everyone.

In the seventh grade we took a state test for geography. If you passed you didn't take the class again. In the eighth grade we took state tests for other subjects. Then you were ready for high school.

CHAPTER TWO
The Old Days at the Kodets

· ·

I remember growing up on a farm with no electricity or running water. We had lamp light. I remember Mother would clean lamp shades once a week, fill all the lamps with kerosene, and trim the wicks. We had a lamp in each bedroom upstairs, and downstairs we had the kitchen light on a side wall with a mirror behind it, but in the dining room we had the Aladdin lamp. It was a lamp with a tall "glass chimney", and it gave a powerful light. Us little kids were not allowed to touch the lamps.

I grew up in a big square two story house that was built in 1926 with a big attic. It has a glassed in porch addition on the east side, and an addition on the north side that included a pantry and entry. There were three bedrooms, a store room upstairs, a kitchen, dining room, living room and a bedroom downstairs. The basement was divided into two rooms. The first room had half of the room on the south side of the stairs filled with corn cobs almost to the ceiling for fuel for the cook stove for winter. The north half had the big canning shelves full of veggies, jams jellies, and fruit sauces, and also canned beef and chicken. There was the potato bin, stored vegetables such as cabbage, carrots, and of course a place for the egg cases, as we

The new barn built in 1925 and the new house built in 1926

had lots of chickens. The second room had the big furnace that was always my Dad's job to fill it, and clean out the ashes. We had a big floor register on the first floor between the living room and the dining room. The south side of that basement room was full of wood that was made on the farm, and the north side had a coal bin. Dad would have his ax and pickax down there to cut up the stumps, and break up the coal. The coal was used for the night fires. There was a door between the two rooms to keep the first room cool. Behind the door in the furnace room was the 55 gallon wooden wine barrel. We had a long line of grapes behind the grove that we picked every year, and Dad would put them through the wine press. No, we did not stomp them with our bare feet.

Before winter came Dad would go to town and buy six or seven hundred pounds of flour, two hundred pounds of sugar, and a big bag of salt, and this would go into the store room upstairs. So we were prepared for winter.

The new barn built in 1925

There were two wells on the farm, one by the windmill, the other by the hog barn that was run by a gas motor. One could also use the pump handle to bring up water, so all water had to be carried into the house. Two pails for drinking water would be set on the pantry table to also be used for cooking. There was a cistern that we would pump soft water to be used for laundry, and put in the stove reservoir to have warm water for dishes and washing.

There was a two car garage not far from the east porch, and behind the garage was the "outhouse", the "air conditioned" bathroom, but in the winter a portable bathroom was set up in the furnace room in the basement.

Electricity finally came to the farm in 1949. Alphonse and I had been married three years by then. One of the first changes was the upstairs store room was changed into a bathroom.

Birth place of Alois E. Kodet, my Dad, February 12,1892 at the Wencel and Mary Kodet farm near Bechyn

CHAPTER THREE
The Old Days on the Kodet Farm

. . . .

My Mother and Dad had a family of nine children, three sons, and six daughters. Emil, then Johanna, Lydia, Edward, Martha, Barbara, (Me), Adella, Mary Lou, and last but not least Alois Jr. I was number six.

My room upstairs had two beds in it, so I shared a room with Johanna, Adella and Mary Lou. We were on the NE corner of the house, so we could look out on the big barn, the old barn, the granary, the hen house, and the other small buildings. We could watch the activity on the farm.

I remember when Mother would varnish the stairway. She was so proud of the way it looked, so she'd varnish it every three or four years to keep it looking good. Varnish at that time was not fast drying, so we could not use the stairs for a couple of days. How we loved that, a ladder would be set up, so we would go up to the roof on the porch, and into a window to get to our rooms.

When I think back, I realize us little kids really used our imaginations. We couldn't wait for Dad, and the boys to shell the corn in the corn crib. When they did we would get brooms, and Adella and I would

Late 1940s, Dad on top of wagon, and Emil on top of corn crib roof.

6

sweep out the one side of the crib, and play house. We'd divide it, and drag boxes, dolls, toy dishes, and stuff out there. Mary Lou always helped too, but Martha was a little older, and she'd come to visit. We'd go out to the tank in the grove where the junk was kept, and bring in cans, and anything we could find to set up our corn crib household. We had a "stove," and "coffee pot," and we would make mud pies, and pretend. Mother, and the older sisters would come, and visit, and we'd serve them pies, and coffee.

One time we went to wash our muddy hands and "kettles," down by the big stock tank. Dad caught us, and really scolded us, he told us that the horses and cows didn't like to drink dirty water, so he gave us a pail to take water out of the tank, and wash up that way. We never washed in the stock tank again. We liked to watch as the horses were led out of the barn, and drank water, so we thought that made sense. We spent a lot of the summer in the corn crib. The breeze would come through, and it was very pleasant. Another thing we'd liked to do is play in the grove. We'd rake the leaves aside, to make roads to drive our wagon on, and rake out big squares, to make farms.

One of my first chores was to bring in cobs and wood to start the cook stove fire in the morning. In the winter I'd go into the basement to get cobs, but otherwise I'd go and pick up cobs by the corn crib, and sticks in the grove. Another chore I

1937 Note the truck in the field.

had was wiping dishes. I'd generally sneak out after dinner, and someone would have to get me from the corn crib, and I would wipe those dishes pretty fast. You can tell I didn't like that job too well.

Another game we liked to play was "Cops and Robbers," or else you could call it, "Cowboys and Indians." Emil had made us some guns out of wood. We would use a rubber band cut from an inner tube, and stretch it on the gun, and there was a trigger of some sort, so we would play in the barn. Someone would be, "IT," and the rest of us would hide. So we could try, and get, "IT." with our guns before they got us. I remember hiding in the horse's manger, under the oats box, and getting, "IT," before they got me. The horses got pretty used to us.

1930's Stacking grain, Martha on the ground. LR: Ed, Emil, Dad on the top of the stack and Johanna.

CHAPTER FOUR
Memories from the Past

. . . .

My Dad's home farm was a mile to the east across the field. Mother's home farm was ¾ mile to the south across the field. To the west of us lived John and Anna Wilt, a short way across the field. Anna was Mom's sister. They were Godparents for all of us kids. Our mail box was next to theirs, so we saw them every day. We would stop at the house, and visit and play with Joe, their adopted son who was a nephew. His mother was John's sister, she had died in childbirth, so they were happy to take the baby. Joe suffered from epilepsy, and later on from rheumatoid arthritis. He was bed ridden for a couple of years before he passed away at the age of twenty two. He was the same age as my brother Ed. When he was bed ridden we would play checkers, Chinese checkers or cards with him.

Dad came from a family of five sisters and four brothers. His Dad owned quite a bit of land, so Dad only went to school at our District 12 for four years. After fourth grade he stayed home, and helped on the farm. Even so he kept educating himself. We always got a daily newspapers, "The Minneapolis Tribune." Mother got her Bohemian newspaper about once a month, so they both kept up with news from the Old Country.

Dad became involved with local proceedings in Henryville Township. He was clerk on the board, and became very busy at certain times when the gravel trucks were hauling gravel. He was a, "Road Boss," so he would check the loads as they were delivered, and supervised the miles to be covered. Then we could figure out all the Sunday afternoon trips around the neighborhood looking at crops, also checking out where gravel was needed. He was also on the school board for District 12. I remember one year it, was probably in the depression, that Dad went to Olivia, and brought home a car load (Model A Ford) of food. It was to be divided to all those in the school district, so he and Mom were weighing out the bulk food, such as rice, beans, sugar, etc. etc. There were also cans of veggies and condensed milk. We always had our own milk and cream, so Mother had to figure out a way to use it.

In our house we had back to back cupboards in the kitchen, and dining room. It was more like a hutch in the dining room with the glass doors above, and a buffet side by side below. There were two deep drawers, and one long shallow drawer at the bottom for table cloths. One big drawer held newspapers, and the one below had games, cards, colors etc. The other two drawers toward the corner of the room were Dad's office. He kept all his ledgers, books, and papers in them. We never opened those drawers, they were off limits, not even to get a pencil or anything. When Dad would do bookwork he had the table close by to spread out his bookwork.

We had a battery radio in a corner of the dining room. It had a big battery like a car battery, and from time to time Dad would take it to town to have it recharged. We listened to the news, country music, "Amos and Andy," etc. Certain nights it was, "Gangbusters," or, "The Lux Presents Hollywood," a movie would burn the air. Always something

My Grandma Kodet, Mary Swovoda feeding the chickens in 1930 born April 01,1861, and died May 1935

interesting on the radio.

On winter nights we would all sit in the dining room. We did our homework. Dad would be in his rocker reading the newspaper, and smoking his one cigar of the day. Mother would sit in her rocking chair, and be crocheting. My older sisters would be embroidering pillow cases, or some fancy work. Then Ed would start the popcorn, and soon we'd all be eating popcorn and apples. Dad was also on the board at North Redwood Farmers Elevator for many years. He was active on church committees at St. Mary's Catholic Church in Bechyn. He also sold Moormans Feed, and Archer Oil.

June 1948 Uncle John Wilt Godfather to all nine of us children

CHAPTER FIVE
The Kodet Farm

. . . .

My Mother, Barbara Kojetin, came from a family of seven sisters, and one brother. Mary, Anna, Josephine, Emma, Barbara, Wencel Jr. Johanna and Angela. Her Dad was born in Chicago, and her Mother, Mary Horesji, came from Bechyne, Czechoslovakia. Her Grandfather, also named Wencel, helped build the first church in Bechyn, and named the town.

Mother went to eight years of school at District 4, ¾ mile to the east, and one mile south. She was eleven years old when she made her first communion at St. Mary's Catholic Church in Bechyn, MN. When she married Dad, in October 29, 1918, influenza was a terrible sickness. Mom's Grandmother, Anna Kojetin had died from the flu, so gatherings were small, just relatives. The reception was at the house.

They settled on the farm just ¾ mile southeast of Bechyn. I still remember that old house. It was small. I remember it being used as a granary after the new house was built. The new house was built in 1926, the new barn in 1925. The new barn had five horse stalls, room for many horses. I remember the team of Grays, Bill and Frank. Then there was Jess and Tom. Tom was the horse we would ride, bare

February 07,1946, Junior on Tom's back

12

backed. Especially my brother Junior. He could ride that horse, stand on him, and sit way back toward the tail. These were the horses we still had after we got the new Case tractor. We still needed them for making hay, and threshing grain, but that's another story.

Monday was always wash day. The night before Mother would fill the copper boiler with cistern water, so it would be ready to heat the next morning. Homemade soap would be cut into small pieces, water added to it, and heated until it became soft. We had a gas motor on our Maytag with a hose. Exhaust would go out the window in the entry. Mom would say, Anna already is washing clothes, as she could hear the motor of her wash machine going. This would be at six o'clock in the morning. Oh! The clotheslines would look so lovely, all those white shirts catching a breeze, and the sheets so white, the towels and dresses, and the jeans and overalls. The men would wear white shirts, and suits to church always. Our dresses were generally hand washed with the tub, and washboard, and a milder soap. Tuesday was ironing day. Mother had gotten another ironing board, and three more sad irons to heat on the stove, so that two of us could iron. The sad irons had a handle that would fit into holes on top of the iron, and a click would lock it in. They would gradually cool as one was ironing, so they had to be changed. We had to be careful, if they were too hot, we would scorch the material. We learned through experience.

With six girls in the house, Mother had to be a good manager, and a good teacher. Saturday was always house cleaning day.

The Kojetin Family, LR: September 10,1950, Mary Kodet, Anna Wilt, Josephine Frank, Emma Halliday, Mother Mary Kojetin, Barbara Kodet, my mother, Wencel Kojetin, Jennie Wertish and Angela Frank.

We would alternate the jobs, and there were many. Windows were washed, inside- woodwork was washed, and pantry shelves were relined with newspaper, except the top shelf. The very top had all sorts of odds and ends, but all the rest had everything removed, and newspaper placed down, and everything put back.

Silverware, and utility drawers were cleaned, and arranged. The basement stairs were swept, and cleaned. The stove was cleaned. There were many jobs. Last of all - all the floors were scrubbed, and sometimes waxed. This was downstairs, the upstairs was done too, but not as thorough. It kept us out of mischief. Mother and Dad would go to town on Saturday afternoon. As we had most of the cleaning done in the morning, we just had dinner dishes to do, but we would fool around having fun, and then one of us would see dust on the road, and we'd have to work fast to get those dishes done before they got home.

Mother was great at sewing. She could look at a dress or shirt, come up with her own pattern, and cut it out of newspaper. She sewed a lot in the winter time. Dad would come home from town with yards and yards of material he had bought. Some of it was pretty fancy, and I remember one dress Mom made for me when I was about six years

Wencel and Mary Kojetin
Mary, Anna, Josephine, Emma, Barbara

The young Wencel Kojetin family. Grandpa Wencel, Mary, Barbara, my mother was the littlest one in this picture, Anna, Josephine, Emma, and Grandma Mary.

old. I would spin around, and the skirt would fly out. She'd make school dresses for us, and shirts for the boys. Out of the scraps, she would make piece quilts. When my twin daughters, Barb and Betty, were growing up, Mom would come, and bring about a dozen dresses she had made for them. Six matching dresses for each Twin. They were so cute, and she'd make shorts

14

for the little boys. How special that was.

I have to write about all the baking that Mother did. She made delicious breads, and Kolachy, and raised donuts, and fry bread. She taught us to make angel food cakes, no mix, with 13 egg whites, and beat and beat and beat with an egg beater, and bake in an oven with just enough cobs, and wood in the stove so it didn't get too hot, and came out with an angel food that was so high. Out of the egg yolks we made noodles. It was great fun growing up.

CHAPTER SIX
Quarantined

. . . .

We are quarantined! There is a sign on our house that says that no one can come or go. It is February of 1936, and the snow banks are so high, and it is a record year of subzero temperatures.

There was an outbreak of scarlet fever in our country school, and we school kids had an enforced vacation for six weeks. I was six years old in the second grade, and I was disappointed because there would be no Valentine's Day party for us.

Mother had us put all our school books in the attic so they would not, "catch the fever." It turned out the school didn't want them back anyway.

I don't remember that any of us kids were very sick except Emil. We had a davenport that opened to a bed in the living room, and so Mother had him there where she could care for him. Dad was also sick that winter suffering from inflammatory rheumatism, and he became bedridden also. His legs were so painful that when he would lay down, a big box was placed over his legs, so that the blankets wouldn't touch them.

October 1925
L-R: Lydia, Emil and Johanna

The Lord sent us two angels that winter. Uncle John Wilt and Wencel Kojetin. One or both would come every day, and help with feeding and watering the livestock, and getting feed ready. It was a stormy month so sometimes they couldn't come. Johanna who was 15 years old, and Ed turned 12 years old in March, did the milking. They milked by hand sitting on a one-legged stool. In the winter time we generally didn't milk that many cows, but each one had to milk 3 or 4 cows. They would bring the milk to the house as the separator was set up in the entry way for the winter. They also did the chicken chores, and picked the eggs.

When Emil and Dad became very sick, the doctor from Morton, Dr. Penhall, was called. He came walking over the snowbanks from Highway 71. It was just a gravel road at that time, but it was plowed out. He gave medicine, and said he was too old to walk that far, and he couldn't come anymore. So the next time the young Dr. James Cosgriff came from Olivia. He came several times to attend to Dad and Emil, and also Mother. He didn't complain about the three mile walk.

Mother was pregnant, due in July. She had been working very hard, caring for the sick, and all of us. She too became ill, and had to rest. Mary Lou was a toddler, she would be three in June, and needed special care. We all tried to be well behaved. Lydia was 13 years old, and would be 14 in August, and she became the chief cook, and Martha was her helper. Lydia also had to learn to bake bread. She went back and forth between the pantry, and the bedroom getting instructions from Mother. Mother was worried about the furnace keeping the house warm. So then Uncle John Wilt, and Uncle Wencel Kojetin, also helped out. They would go to the basement by the side door. They also took the cream and eggs to town, and that was quite a job. Everything had to go by sled over the snowbanks. Mother had a list ready, and they brought back some groceries.

What a long, tough winter that was!!!! Dad was slowly getting better, and trying to walk pushing a kitchen chair in front of him. The doctor said his illness as caused by diseased tonsils. So wouldn't you know- we all had our tonsils taken out that spring. Two by two, up to Dr. Cosgriff's clinic, up about 40 or 50 steps above the bank.

SPRING FINALLY CAME!

The driveway was shoveled out, and the sun thawed the snow. Dad and Emil were getting healthier every day.

After a flurry of house cleaning, and washing germs away, we went back to school.

Crops were planted, and then the drought. The summer was so hot. July set record temperatures that haven't been beat to this day. Many days were over 100.

And that was when my baby brother was born. Grandpa and Grandma Kojetin came out in the morning. Grandma was going to stay, but Grandpa was taking Mary Lou, Adella and Me for the day. Grandpa Kojetin always brought chocolate star candy every time he came, so we loved to see him. He took us to his house in Bechyn, and then we went to visit our little Kojetin cousins out at the home farm where Uncle Wencel and Aunt Katie and children lived. He took us home around four o'clock in the afternoon, and the doctor was just leaving. We were so happy to see our

new baby brother, Alois Jr. to be called Junior. It was July 16, 1936. We all loved him so, and tried very hard to "spoil" him. On such a hot day with no electricity, I wonder how anyone kept cool.

I don't know how the crops turned out that year, but the doctor's diagnosis for Dad must have been very correct, as he never had

The Alois and Barbara Kodet Family August 18,1939, LR: Back row, Dad, Mother, Martha, Lydia, Johanna and Emil. Front row, L-R: Adella, Mary Lou, Barbara, Ed and Alois Jr. (Junior)

another attack of inflammatory rheumatism again.

What I know about scarlet fever isn't much, but there was a fever, and a rash. The throat would become very sore, and also the mouth would be full of sores. It would be difficult to eat except for broth or thin soup.

A few years later Highway 71 was tarred. Dad was so excited about it. 71 WAS GETTING TARRED!! HALLELUJAH!!

CHAPTER SEVEN
The Wooden Box

. . . .

In our upstairs storeroom sat a big wooden box about the size of a full sized mattress. It sat on edge, so it didn't take up that much room. In the spring Mother and Dad would set it up in the store room. I don't know if they put it on a saw horse, or if it had legs that folded. It was an incubator. It had two doors that folded down in front. Then in each door was a tray that rolled out. On these trays Mother would place chicken eggs. It held a lot of eggs, possibly a whole case which was thirty dozen. There was a kerosene lamp that was built into the end, and the heat was adjusted by turning the wick up or down. I don't know what temperature was needed to hatch these eggs. Every day for three weeks Mother would sprinkle the eggs with warm water, and she tenderly turn them slightly. She would do this every morning, and evening, and always checked the temperature and the lamp.

In three weeks the baby chicks started popping out of the shell-- what a peep-peep that was. The chicks were so cute and fluffy.

The brooder house was ready for them. The brooder house was a small building heated by a kerosene brooder stove. The stove had a hood over it like an umbrella. The special baby chick feed was already in small feeders, and the water fountains were ready. The baby chicks were placed in a special cardboard ring around the stove that kept them near the heat. As they grew the ring was expanded until it was removed. The stove was no longer needed. The chick door was opened, and they were able to go outside. Then the feed and water was placed outside. When they grew up they were placed in the chicken coop. Most of the roosters had been made into delicious chicken dinners.

In later years Dad built another hen house just east of the windmill. Then they would order baby chicks from Snow's Hatchery in Sleepy Eye, MN. and they were delivered by them. At first the chickens were a heavy breed called Plymouth Rock. The hens would get, "clucky" in the spring, and try to hide their eggs in a nest somewhere outside. They would later come with a brood of baby chicks. We had a special little pen for them something like a calf hutch, called a, "butka." We would set it over the top of them to protect them from the weather. I remember when a new breed of chicken was introduced called the, "Leghorn." They were a smaller chicken, ate less feed, and laid more eggs. After that we always raised Leghorns for hens, and the Plymouth Rock for broilers.

In later years, Alphonse and I also ordered our baby chicks from Snow's Hatchery in Sleepy Eye.

But those hens could be a problem. As they roamed around the yard, they loved green grass. Mother would get upset because they ate all the grass in front of the house. The lawn was lush and green behind the house, but not in front. Mother thought we should have a lawn fence. Dad thought it wasn't necessary, but you know how that goes......... She brought the subject up a "few times." This went on for a couple of years, until Dad finally gave in.

Dad told Mom to figure out what was needed, and he would buy it. Only two sides were needed, as the garden on the west side was already fenced in, and the grove on the south end didn't need to be fenced.

Mother measured, and she figured out how many posts, how much fencing was needed with two sets of double gates so they could get close to the house with racks full of wood, coal, corn cobs, potatoes etc. Mother helped Dad, Emil and Ed install the fence, and how beautiful the lawn was. Along the fence line was a strip of soil especially for flowers.

Flowers of all kinds- peonies, iris, phlox, carnations, roses, geraniums, and many annuals were planted each year. There were always sweet peas climbing up the fence. The more you picked them- the more they bloomed, so we always had a bouquet in the house.

The garden on the west side of the house was always early. The sun would warm the protected spot, and seeds would sprout, and grow fast. Along the grove was the

1949- The house with the fence that Mother wanted so bad. The house was built in 1926

big raspberry patch that Mother said started with six plants. It was bedded down with straw, so that the weeds wouldn't grow. There were always a couple of rows of poppies that would bloom so pretty, and they would produce poppy seed for the Kolachy that Mother used to bake. There were a couple rows of early potatoes, and many times we had a special treat by the 4th of July, tomatoes. She would plant tomato seeds directly into the soil, and by transplanting time, they would be really strong and vigorous plants.

But the big garden was out in the field along the pasture fence. All the melons, squash, pumpkin, sweet corn, tomatoes, and the big strawberry patch. It was always a lot of work keeping the weeds pulled, but the strawberry patch kept us busy. We would pick berries, and eat delicious sauce mixed with berries, peaches, bananas and cream for our enjoyment, and jams and jellies. Many of the strawberries and raspberries were taken to the grocery store, and sold. Mother would order special boxes, and cases in which we placed the berries, and they were ready for display. Dad's sister, Ella would come and spend one day. She didn't help us pick, but she helped make the sauce, and jam. We sent her home with lots of goodies. The money that Mother got for the berries was kept especially for a great shopping trip for all of us "pickers."

The big potato patch was put in a different spot each year. That also had to be weeded, and hoed, but the boys helped get in on that. In the fall Dad had one of the horses hitched to the potato plow, and opened the rows. We would pick the potatoes, and put them on a hay rack. After they dried on the rack a week or so they were put in the potato bin in the basement. They would keep nicely till spring, but by then they were almost used up.

CHAPTER EIGHT
Fishing

. . . .

We're going fishing!! How we loved to hear those words. It was always exciting to go fishing at the creek. Beaver Creek would run through the pasture on Dad's home farm. We'd run down the hill through the prairie grass, there was the creek. Dad's sister Ella, still lived in the brick house there, and we'd always visit with her, and she would fish with us. We had our bamboo rods, and we baited them with angleworms. We had dug them up that morning by pushing aside the straw in the raspberry patch, and found moist ground underneath full of worms. We would catch perch and bullheads and put them into our pail that we brought along with us. A few times our lines got tangled in a branch overhead.

Mother had packed a picnic lunch, so we picked a shady spot, and sat on the grass to eat our meal. We could still watch our bobbers in the water. When we left, Ella gave us her fish too. She said she could fish anytime. Then we piled into our Model A Ford, and Mother drove us all home. We wished Dad could have come too, but he was busy farming, but we all enjoyed the fish fry. It was so peaceful by the water, and such a pleasant memory many years later.

Early 1920's, Dad's sisters Katie and Ella

24

When Alphonse and I took our family to the creek to fish, we still visited with Ella, and she joined us fishing. We wanted our kids to have that pleasant memory also. The hill with the prairie grass was still there, and the creek hadn't changed, and yes we caught fish too.

As I write my memories I have to include the special place that St. Mary's, our church, in Bechyn had in our family. Bechyn was settled by Bohemians that came from the town of Bechyne, Czechoslovakia, in Bohemia. In fact my Great Grandfather, Wencel Kojetin, named the town. His son, also named Wencel, was my Grandfather. He was married to my Grandmother, Mary Horesjsi, who came from Bechyne, Czechoslovakia, when she was sixteen years old. They were married at St. Mary's church in Bechyn, MN. On May 18, 1891. The first church was started in 1879, with Masses in homes. In 1880, a church was built, but by 1890, a larger church was needed. It was in 1915, a new church finally was built, and the old church was moved to be a hall in Bechyn. My Uncle, George Halliday was one of the carpenters, and there is a picture of him standing on top of the steeple holding his arms like a cross. There were beautiful altars and beautiful stained glass windows that were donated by members. We always had a priest that could speak Bohemian, and I remember many sermons that were spoken in Bohemian. The cemetery was next to the church. The season of Lent was faithfully observed by all the people by attending the Stations of the Cross, and Holy Week services. I remember

My Grandparents wedding day,
Wencel and Mary Horesji Kojetin
May 18, 1891

that we kids would always give up candy for Lent. It was given to us, but we would put it away, and hide our "stash." It wasn't until Easter Sunday that we would bring it out, and start eating it. It was in Lent that we always made sure to say the family rosary every day. As we were kneeling, sometimes we would get the giggles, and then Dad would give us the, "look," so we would try to stop. We wouldn't dare look at Ed as he generally got us started. We always had new Easter dresses, and hats to observe the occasion.

After Mass most of the people would go to one of two stores in Bechyn, Charlie's or George's. Each store had a line of chairs to sit on for the ladies, and the young people gathered into groups. I'm sure all the news was hashed and rehashed. Before we'd go home Mother would buy some bologna for an easy Sunday dinner. Everyone had a bologna dinner that day. Good sales for the stores.

For two weeks every summer we would have vacation school with the Notre Dame Nuns as teachers. They would prepare us for First Communion or Confirmation, and teach us about our Catholic religion. We always enjoyed that. We would carpool with the neighbors. In those days there was a lot of support in that little town. Grandpa and Grandma Kojetin retired to a nice home in Bechyn which still stands today. It has been added onto, and kept in good repair by a young couple.

Bechyn had a baseball team that played mostly on Sunday afternoons. Joe and Clarence Serbus, my brother-in-laws, were on the team. There was always horseshoe players using the stakes. Cards were played inside the two stores every Sunday evening. Wedding dances, and wedding showers

Kodet Brother's Band. My Dad on the drums. Adolph, Alois and Joe

26

were held in the hall, and many meetings, also elections for Henryville Township. One of the bands playing at the dances was the Kodet Family Band. Our Dad played the drums, and his brothers, Joe and Adolph both played the concertinas.

In later years my sisters and I were members of the choir, and we had practice on Wednesday nights. When Alphonse, and I were dating (we had no phones,) if he came on Wednesday night he'd find me at choir practice. Then we'd all end up going to the movies or get together at someone's home.

CHAPTER NINE
Armistice Day Blizzard

· ·

November 11, 1940, was the date of the, "STORM OF THE CENTURY IN MINNESOTA." It was a Monday following a week of mild weather. It began with rain, and then sleet, and as the temperature dropped it turned to snow. My sister, Martha, got on the bus at 7am at the end of the driveway to Olivia High School. Cousin, Edmund Kodet, was already on the bus. Our brother, Ed, was going to agriculture school in Morris, Minnesota at the time. The bus driver crossed Highway 71, and picked up a couple more students. The snow was coming down so heavy he decided to head to town. Visibility was getting so bad, the wind so strong. He took eight kids to the rest home where his Mother lived. He knew the school would be closed. The storm raged for two days before the wind died down. Martha and another girl would sleep on a couch that opened into a bed. Time moved slowly, but they were all grateful to be safe inside a warm place. They kept busy visiting the old folks.

When the storm was over, Martha and Edmund walked uptown to our uncle and aunt's, at the, "Halliday's Grocery Store."

The snow was so deep, and the drifts were so high. Everyone was shoveling snow. Uncle George and Aunt Emma Halliday had received a phone call that our Grandpa Kojetin had died during the storm. They were going to try to get to Bechyn. Grandpa was 74 years old. Martha and Edmund were welcome to stay at their house with the rest of the family until someone came to get them. It was a couple of more days before Mother and Dad could get them, and then it was Grandpa's wake and funeral. The wake was at their home in Bechyn. There was so much deep snow all over, the drifts were as high as the telephone poles. I don't remember much about the funeral, so I don't know if they were able to bury him in the cemetery that day, but I do remember the wake. In a home wake there is someone who stays awake all night, and keeps vigil over the body of the loved one. We stayed until about midnight, Dad, Mom and her sisters and brother stayed all night. I remember that the big Grandfather clock had been stopped at the time of his death. Grandpa wouldn't come to visit anymore, and bring us chocolate star candy, but maybe he is passing it out in heaven. That Monday morning at the farm we were rescuing chickens that had roosted in the trees in the warm weather. It was raining, and starting to sleet and snow, and the chickens didn't want to move. As they flew down we would catch them, and carry them to the hen house. By the time we finished it was snowing very hard, and the wind was strong. Our country school started at 9am in the winter, so with the storm we didn't go to school. We worried about Martha, and wondering where she was.

Dad and Emil were doing extra livestock chores getting ready for the storm. And what a storm it was!! The wind was so bad, and the temperature went way down. We were in a warm house with plenty of wood and coal, and plenty of food, so we were okay.

I went to the library, and got a book to research the storm, and I found out why it was called, "The Storm of the Century." There were 59 people in Minnesota that lost their lives that day. Many were deer hunters or duck hunters. Many were people who left their cars that had gotten stuck on the road, and left to walk to shelter. Some stayed in their cars, and the snow had completely covered the car. The wind was a steady 36 miles an hour wind with gusts up to 60 miles per hour. Snow piled up from 16 inch snowfall in some places to as high as a 26 inch snowfall in places. Some highways had 15 foot drifts on them. It took weeks to shovel out. Some home owners had to go out a window on the sheltered side of the house in order to shovel out their doors.

Strangely enough there wasn't too much of snowfalls the rest of the winter until another blizzard on St. Patrick's (March 17), 1941. What a coincidence that there was another St. Patrick's blizzard in 1965. That year Mike was born, and we had to get to the hospital in that blizzard.

There was a lot of snow in 1936 also, the winter we were quarantined, but that winter was so much colder. There was a stretch of 42 consecutive days that the temperature didn't get above zero. Minnesota weather is unpredictable. There was no weather forecasts about the coming storm.

Junior clearing snow from the yard. February 21,1952 when we had a tractor on the farm

That Monday morning at the Mages farm about 20 miles away south of the Minnesota River, (this was before I met Alphonse, but he told this to me,) was also a busy one getting the livestock ready for the coming storm. It was beginning to sleet when their Dad, Oswald told Alphonse, almost 12 years old, and brother Albin, almost 13 years old to go to the pasture to bring the horses to the barn. There was a straw pile at the far end of the pasture, and the five or six horses were huddled there. They would get them away from the straw pile, but they would always run back. After several times of trying to herd the horses to the barn, they had trouble seeing them. It was snowing so hard, and the wind was strong. The horses would not leave the straw pile.

Visibility was getting bad, and soon they were lost in the storm. They didn't know if they were going the right way, but then they hit the barbed wire fence. They followed the fence going against the wind. At times the wind was so strong they couldn't move. At last they could get to the barn, and then to the house. Their Mother and Dad had been so worried about them, and were so glad to see them.

After the storm was over they went to see about the horses. They had burrowed into the straw stack, and were okay, but the steers that had taken refuge in the drainage ditch were all dead. The snow had covered them up, and smothered them. There were many turkey farmers that had turkeys that were on the range that were ready for market that lost all their turkeys, thousands of them. Now turkeys are raised in big barns, but at the time, "on the range," meant in open alfalfa fields. They had shelters for sun, and rain that had a long sloping roof on which they would roost at night. Many of those turkey would have gone to market that week because Thanksgiving was coming.

We have had blizzards since then that have been very serious. We have more sophisticated weather forecasting now. We have more and better snow plows, and we have snowmobiles. (Quote from Mike, my son.) When he had to talk about his patron saint in St. Mary's School when he was in third or fourth grade, Michael Patrick told of being born on St. Patrick's Day in the blizzard of 1965, and he was so serious when he ended his story saying, "They didn't have any snowmobiles then." Mike's teacher shared that.

CHAPTER TEN
Harvest Time

· ·

The old house was coming down! It had been used as a small granary, and a place to keep seeds and feeds. There was to be a new granary built on the spot. Dad had hired a carpenter from Bechyn, Frank Malecek, to oversee the project. All the digging trenches for the foundation was done by hand. It would have bins on both sides, a drive through shed for machinery in the middle, and overhead bins on the top. Those could be emptied by driving the truck underneath, and opening a trap door. All the cement work was done on the spot. Sand was hauled in, and mixed with cement and water in the cement mixer, and hauled away with wheelbarrows. Dad would also have medium rocks that he would drop into the trenches here and there into the cement. It turned out to be a big building, and Dad, Emil and Ed painted it red with white trim. What a beautiful addition to our yard.

It was to be very useful as much of the farm was planted into grain crops such as oats, wheat and flax. Soybeans were still a crop of the future.   Have you ever seen a field of flax in bloom? It is a spectacular, and beautiful sight. The flowers are so blue, it looks like a huge lake. My Dad grew flax every year. In fact he became quite an authority on the subject. His field always looked so wonderful. His secret was: After the field was planted he went over it with a packer. I think they call it a roller now days. As the crop matured each blossom became a little ball of seed. Dad sold a lot of the crop as seed to other farmers. In fact Oswald Mages came to buy some flax seed, and of course Alphonse came with him. Flax seed is very slippery. We were warned to never go into a bin of Flax as we would sink in it, and not be able to get out. That was why there were always several wide boards on top of the flax just in case.

Harvest was the busiest time of the year. After the grain was ripe it was cut into bundles, and shocked. Dad, Emil and Ed would put the tractor on the grain binder, and open the field. The sickle cut the grain, and it was tied into a bundle. When the bundle carrier held about six to eight bundles Dad would drop them in a row, so they could be stood up and shocked. Two this way, two more that way, and adding around the shock. Opening the fields was the hardest part as you had to drive the first round on the grain. All the bundles had to be carried out of the way, so the back swath could be taken. After that I was the tractor driver for Dad, so Ed and Emil could shock the oats, wheat or flax. Mother and Johanna, and the other sisters also got in on it. I would too when the field was all down, and I would help finish up. These shocks would sit in the field at least a week or longer until dry enough to be threshed.

Dad owned the threshing machine, and so he organized the threshing ring. Neighboring farmers also needed their shocks threshed, so from one farm to another farm threshing was done until it was finished. Emil was the machine man. He took care of the greasing, and oiling the machine. There was a long belt from the tractor to the machine to run the big pulley on the machine. When we did our fields, Dad and Johanna hauled the grain to the elevator, or unloaded it in the granary. It also involved a lot of labor. It was very difficult during the war years as many sons were serving in the Armed Forces. Dad had two hired men that came up from Iowa for two or three weeks each year to help out. That was also when we older girls had to learn how to spick bundles with our pitchforks, so the load wouldn't slide out before it got to the threshing machine. We didn't drive the horses or unload at the machine, but we were, "spike pitchers." We helped any driver load his bundles so the machine would keep going.

This is where the horses came in handy. Each farmer had at least two teams, and racks to haul bundles to the machine to keep it going. Four farmer- eight teams of horses. Later on there were three farmers in the ring. If it was a long haul, more teams were needed. Some would need the straw stack in the cow yard, or sometime it was left out in the field. Many times all the horses stayed overnight in a stall in the barn.

But Mother needed the help also, It took a lot of food to feed these hungry crews. For morning lunch, dinner, afternoon lunch, and supper. Special breads, and desserts were made, chicken was ready to fry, veggies and salads were prepared. Water, soap and towels were set up on a bench outside on the cistern cement, and they all washed up before coming in to the house to eat. The dining room table was full of men laughing and joking.

After the season, Dad and Mother would throw a party for all the families, and crew. He'd get a keg of beer, and Mother would prepare a big feed. Dad passed around his home made wine to the women. This one family had a Mother, and two daughters that didn't drink wine, so the next year Dad asked them if they'd like grape juice, and they did take some. When he came around the second time they wanted a refill so he thought he'd better not do that again. He didn't want them to get too much of that, "grape juice."

Corn harvest came later in the fall. There was also a corn binder that made corn bundles. The bundles were hauled in, and stacked beside the hog and steer yard. They were used for winter feed. The corn that wasn't cut for the stack was piled, and stored in the corn crib. That is where the horse came into use again. Ed and I had a team, and a rack that had boards nailed on the far side to make a bang board. The idea was to hit the bang board, and not overshoot the rack with the ears of corn. Dad and Johanna had a team also. Ed and I started out first on these one half mile rows. At first he'd help me keep up, but I got better after a while. Dad and Johanna came after us. We all wore a leather strap around our left wrist that had a hook on it. We'd grab the husk, hook the husk open, and snap the ear, and throw it at the bang board. Ed would give a short, "git" or whistle, and the horses would move up a bit. After a while they caught on, and as we moved up, they did too. When we got to the end, we turned around, and put on two more rows of corn, by then it was noon. Ed would drive into the double corn crib, and start unloading, and soon Dad and Johanna would come with their load. After dinner we went out, and did two more loads. So it went till the field was finished. By then Emil was married, and was on his own farm, and Lydia was also married, and living on a farm not too far away.

CHAPTER ELEVEN
World War II

· ·

The year is 1941. Farmers are beginning to recover from the Great Depression of the 1930's, when corn was eight cents a bushel, and livestock prices were just as bad. Alphonse used to tell the story of the farmers that had a load of market lambs taken to South St. Paul. By the time he paid the trucker, the yardage at the stockyard, he still owed money, so he said, and "I have another load at home ready to go."

My Dad bought a new car, a two tone light, and dark Chevrolet sedan. It was a beautiful car, as modern as the gear shift was under the steering wheel. We still kept the Model A, especially for going in the field. Emil had his car also, a light brown two door Chevrolet, so we generally were a two car family driving to church. Dad had his truck that he hauled grain to the elevator. He was on the board at the North Redwood Elevator, so he hauled grain to them. He'd always take the dog along. One time the dog got out of the truck, and Dad couldn't find him, so he left him, as he was coming back the next day. When Blackie heard the truck the next day, he came running, and Dad opened the door, and Blackie jumped in.

It was a shock to all in the Bechyn community when Pearl Harbor was attached by the Japanese on December 07, 1941. It was a Sunday, and we were listening to the radio for any news, so war was declared soon after. We were at war with both Japan and Germany. Many young men joined the service right away. Many more waited to be drafted into the service. There were many ratings by the Draft Board. 1A meant you went right away. 2A meant you were deferred for essential jobs. 2S you were deferred for college. 4F meant you were physically unable to serve. We thought Ed would be considered 4F because of his eyesight. When he was about five years old Mother and Dad took him to Minneapolis for eye surgery. He always wore corrective glasses, and he would joke, "That he was blind in one eye, and he couldn't see out of the other."

Ed was drafted, and given a desk job so most of the war he spent in Hawaii at the army base there. Emil was considered a farmer, and needed at home for the war effort.

We lived on a farm, and had our own milk, eggs, meat so we didn't have the hardships that some people had. We were given ration books that we could redeem coupons for sugar, coffee, butter and meat. Tires and gasoline were also rationed. The speed limit was reduced to forty miles per hour. The rubber tires weren't that good, so slower speed limits helped wear on the tires.

Martha and I were going to Olivia High School for the 1942 school year. At Christmas time we were told buses would not pick us up unless we went to a pick up farther away, and Dad said he didn't get enough gas to haul us there, so we didn't go any more. The following year I went to high school in Olivia. I stayed at Uncle George and Aunt Emma Halliday's home, and I went home on the weekends. Then the Morton superintendent came out, and put us in Morton jurisdiction, and from then on we went to Morton High School. The bus picked us up at our driveway.

Lydia had gotten married that summer to Joe Serbus, and they lived on a farm about four miles away. Then in January Emil was married to Rosella Bartes, quite a coincidence as they had birthdays close together, and they were baptized the same day. When Lydia got married I moved into her room, and now I shared a room with Martha. We took turns making breakfast,

Martha did a week, and I did a week. We would get up early, and have to start a fire in the cook stove. First we'd get the special wrench, and shake the ashes down. There was a drawer under the firebox to catch the ashes, and would have to be emptied if it was full. Then we could start the fire. When I got the fire started I would turn on the radio, and get country music. It was June 06, 1944, and I could get nothing on the radio except static. Actually it was long range radio broadcasting. It was D-Day in Europe. I called Dad right away, and he started listening. Our army was landing on the beach at Normandy in France, and the German Army was fighting back. It was the beginning of many battles across Europe.

By this time Clarence Serbus was fighting in the Japanese theater, He was engaged to my sister, Martha. Alphonse's brother Albin was in Europe. He and my sister, Adella, were exchanging many letters, and later married. Many of my cousins were fighting in combat. Many, many prayers were being said for all our young men.

Factories were all turned over to making armor for the war, tanks, guns, ammunition, battleships, airplanes etc. Farm machinery, cars, appliances were not made. Even clothing and shoes were hard to get. Such things as sheets or bath towels were on the hard to get list. Syrup was used instead of sugar, and I remember if you were able to buy a pair of nylon stockings you were very lucky. Even after the war was over the shortages lasted several years. If you wanted to buy a tractor, or a car you put your name on a list.

In May of 1945, World War II in Europe was over. Many prisoners of war were rescued, and also people in the concentration camps. So, much of Europe had been destroyed by all the bombing, and it was going to be an overwhelming job to rebuild.

The war with Japan continued as our Armed Forces were conquering islands that could be used as air bases, but there was so much loss of life. In August of 1945, an atomic bomb was dropped on Hiroshima, Japan, and then three days later another bomb on Nagasaki, Japan. The Japanese surrendered officially on September 02, 1945, on the U.S.S. Missouri in Tokyo Bay

THE WAR WAS OVER, THANK GOD!!!!

It took a while for the young men to come home. They stayed for occupation. Albin came home the beginning of October 1946, and Clarence Serbus came home the end of October, 1946. He came home the night of our wedding dance when Alphonse and I got married, October 29, 1946. Brother Ed came back from Hawaii in the early fall of 1946. His hair that use to be straight had turned curly, no matter how many haircuts he had. It was so good to have all the young men home again. Martha was married to Clarence next January 14, 1947.

May 1945, L-R: Mary Lou, Martha, Ed, Barbara and Adella

CHAPTER TWELVE
Chicken Dinner

. . . .

Every year Mother would raise many young chickens as broilers. They would be sold to make tasty chicken dinners for many people. BUT, during the summer chicken was our tasty dinner. Every morning when either Martha or I were making breakfast, Mother would be out getting chickens butchered, and cleaned for our noon meal. Then the chickens would be in cold water until time to prepare it. We had fried chicken, roasted chicken, creamed chicken, broiled chicken, broasted chicken, boiled chicken, cold chicken, chicken soup, chicken with noodles, chicken with rice, chicken salad, Kodet fried chicken, Bechyn fried chicken, canned chicken, sandwiches made with chicken, and to think – we never got tired of eating chicken. It is still one of my favorite foods.

(This reminds me of Bubba on the movie, "Forest Gump," describing all the ways you can prepare shrimp. Mom and I had a good laugh over this while I'm typing this.) On Saturday Mother would prepare extra chicken that she roasted for Sunday. Dad always had a drumstick before he went to bed.

When cool weather came, Dad, Emil and Ed would butcher a hog. Much preparation was needed. A block and tackle was put in a strong branch of a tree on the edge of the grove. A barrel of hot water was ready, and a make shift table of boards to lay the hog on. Knives were sharpened on the grindstone. They would scrape the hair off the skin after the hog was scalded in the hot water. When the scraping was done the hog was covered with a clean sheet, and raised up as high as they could, and it was cooled overnight. It was raised very high in the tree so no other animal would come, and eat the meat during the night. The next day was a very busy one for all of us in the house. Dad quartered the hog, and brought in a quarter at a time. Mother would cut the meat up, and brown it on the cook stove in two large pans that just fit into the oven. After the meat was browned she roasted it in the oven, and then removed it and put it in a 20 gallon crock jar.

She had trimmed the lard off the meat, so we girls had our bread boards on the dining room table, and we would cube the lard, so it could be rendered later. After all four quarters were done, the rendered lard would be poured over the meat in the crock until it was covered. This meat would keep under the lard until it was used up. That was usually our meat for supper meals. We had a special roaster pan for this meat, and would warm it up in the oven.

Mother would make "jitternice" out of the hog head. Boil it, and mix it with liver, onions, pearl barley, bread crumbs, some garlic and seasoning. This was made into sausage for a tasty treat.

In the winter time hams and bacon were smoked in Dad's smokehouse.

A steer was butchered in the winter time. As we had no electricity our cooler was the enclosed east porch. It was cold enough to freeze the meat out there. Dad would go out with his meat saw, and we kids would watch through the window. He had asked Mother what she wanted, and if she wanted enough for four or five days. He would cut off a big chunk, and when it thawed Mother would cut it as she wanted it.

Mother would also can some of the beef. It was very good for a quick meal. Dad had a grinder, and he would grind some into hamburger. The grinder was always ran by, "elbow grease."

After I was married a couple of years, butcher shops in town would offer, "lockers" to people. You could bring your quarters of meat into the butcher shop, and they would cut and package it for you, and place it in a storage box called a locker. Once a week we could go, and take as many packages as we'd need until the next time. That way we always had fresh meat. When deep freezers became available that also was a change, as we could store our meat at home. We could butcher chickens at our convenience, and also freeze our garden vegetables, and fruit, our baked goods such as bread, cakes, cookies, and best of all ICE CREAM!!!!!!!!

Every winter Dad would put an order to Morley Fish Company from Duluth, Minnesota, for fresh fish, and salted herring. The fish would come fresh out of the water, still had their heads on, but they were degutted. The scales had to be scraped off them. Never

1940,L-R: Ed, Emil, George Halliday Jr., Junior, Dad, George Halliday Sr. Pheasant and duck hunting, note the windmill on the right used to run water into the tank for the animals.

heard of filleting a fish at that time. Dad would bring in the fish on Thursday night after supper, and he would clean them, so they would be ready for the Friday dinner. We would be very careful not to eat the fish bones, but they were very delicious. Another thing Dad always had on hand was horehound candy. You younger people probably never heard of it. It had a distinct flavor-something like a cough drop.

Grandpa Wencel and Grandma Mary Kodet home

March 13, 1952, Junior and Dad butching a hog

CHAPTER THIRTEEN
Milking Cows

One of my summertime chores was milking cows, by hand. We had a Red Shorthorn herd of cows, maybe twenty head. Dry cows, and milking cows. They were supposed to be easy milkers, easier than Holsteins. Ed and Johanna usually milked in the morning, but Ed would help Dad during the day with farm work, so I'd help Johanna with evening chores. About three fourths of the barn on the north side was cow pens, and the rest was for the calves. There were no stanchions, so we would carry our one-legged stool, and sit down by the cow, and milk away. If the cow was a little nervous, she would walk away a little, but I'd wait until she settled down. When it was very hot, we would carry our stools, and sit down with our cows right in the cow yard. Each one of us would milk four or five cows.

The cream separator was set up in the new granary by the east door. We would carry our pails of milk there, and pour the milk into a big strainer into the big separator bowl. It held a big pail of milk. The separator was a heavy implement with a big spout for the milk, and a smaller spout for cream. The milk would run from the big bowl on top into the discs that would separate the milk from the cream. We would set a pail under each spout to catch the skim milk, and cream. It was a two man job, or a two woman job. There was a handle that would turn the whole mechanism, and you would have to turn the handle fast until you got, "up to speed," and then turn the petcock that would let the milk run out of the big bowl.

The speed would have to be on high until all the pails of milk were separated. The one that kept refilling the big bowl, and switching pails under the spouts was also very busy. When all the milk was done, water would be used to rinse out all the parts to clean them.

The skim milk would be fed to the calves, and or the pigs. The cream would be taken to the cooler, and added to the cream can that was already there. It would be sold later. The cooler sat between the windmill, and the big stock tank. It was round, generally make of cedar or redwood with a pipe going in coming from the windmill pump. It was large enough to hold three or four milk cans. There was a pipe going out on the other side to the big stock tank. The water was constantly changing as long as the windmill turned. When the stock tank got full the windmill was turned off. There was a cover on the cooler. Half of the cover could be raised at a time. One can would hold cream, and one can would hold butter, jars of cream, and milk. These were used in the house. Another can would hold bottles of beer, and pop for the harvest workers.

In the wintertime the separator was moved into the entry way in the house. The separator dishes would have to be washed every day.

When I was married, Dad and Mother gave me two cows, and a yearling heifer. I named the cows Mary Ann and Betty. Alphonse got six cows from his parents, and we named them Lucy, Dusty,

Dad with the DC Case

Blackie, Gertie, Whitey and Kicker. We milked by hand for one year before we got an electric, "Surge," milk machine because they had a Surge milk machine at his parents, and it was "the best."

45

We had an electric motor on our cream separator, so no more handle turning. That was so neat, but those dishes still had to be washed every day.

Dusty was a great cow, as she had two sets of twins. Lucy also filled that Surge bucket every time, and her calves were mostly heifer calves.

When I went to Morton High School, I took typing class with the sophomores, as I never had typing. One of my classmates was Dorothea Scheffler (Paul.) We also rode on the same bus, so I knew her well. We would compete against each other, as we learned to type. We were neck and neck for most of the year, and we became very good typists, (without mistakes.) I wish I had that skill today. Anyway Dorothea also milked cows by hand, and she would say, "We were good at typing because we milked by hand." Dorothea would go on to become one of our great Minnesota artists painting pictures of farming in the past days, and tractors and horses. Dorothea painted a picture for our 60th wedding anniversary that had been commissioned by our family. It was a picture of Alphonse and mine's original farm site where we first lived by Morton, MN. It was a picture of picking corn in the fall with tractors in the field, and unloading corn into the corn cribs. Children were on the sand pile, some on a motor scooter. The cows were in the cow yard, and hogs and chickens in their yard. The pumpkins were orange in the garden, and flowers blooming by the house. The leaves on the trees were turning color. It was a great painting.

CHAPTER FOURTEEN
My Grandmas

. . . .

My Grandma Kojetin, Mary Horesji, almost made 100 years. She died in April of 1970, and she would have been 100 on September 10th. She was born in Bohemia, Czechoslovakia, in the town of Bechyne. She was a young girl of sixteen when she came to America. Her ship was almost hit by an iceberg, so it was a scary trip for her, and her younger brother John Horesji.

I'll always remember her for her green thumb. She could grow the best garden, and she did that well into her nineties. She lived in Bechyn, Minnesota, a name given by her father-in-law Wencel Kojetin, to this little town and church. They say if you blink an eye as you're driving through you might miss it. We stopped every Sunday after church, and visited for a while. We'd always go to look at her garden. When the peas were ready to eat, she'd encourage us to go pick them and eat. I've grown peas for many years, and never did I have peas as tall, and productive as hers. That was every year. I think she saved her own seed, you can't even buy it anymore. My Mother also saved her own seed for peas, beans, onions, carrots, tomatoes, cucumbers, melons, squash, Most Everything. Now days with hybrid seeds, we don't get good crops if we save seed. I do know Gedney had very good cucumber seed the three years Alphonse and I grew cucumbers for the factory. From one half acre the first year, one and one half acres the second year, and two acres the third year. It was back breaking work, but quite an experience. Couldn't have done it without the help of the kids. I think after three years, they all had enough. RIGHT!!!!!!!!!!!!!!!!!!!!!!!!!!!!

Back to Grandma, she also had many flowers blooming outside, and house plants too. She had an enclosed porch on the south side of the house with tables full of blooming flowers, especially Gloxinias. Gloxinias are a bell shaped blossom in colors of red, pink, purple bordered by white. A very showy flower that seemed to bloom all the time. She also had African Violets and ferns of all kinds, and geraniums.

Grandma never learned to speak English. After being in this country for so many years, I think she knew a lot of English. By not speaking English, we were forced to converse with her in Bohemian, and we kids could understand better than we could speak it. So we tried to talk to her in our broken Bohemian. We could pray, "Svathe Maria, Matka Boyse," or we could count to one hundred. I can still do that—slowly, or we could sing a simple song, or remember our toast, "Na zdrowie."

We'll always remember Grandma for her baking skills. She made delicious bread, and coffee cakes, and she always had cookies for us kids to eat.

Grandma was a tall lady, but very slender. She lost a few inches in her height in her later years. Grandpa was six feet, and she was almost as tall. She had long hair that she would roll into a knot on the back of her head, but in later years, she had shoulder length hair. She always wore long dresses, and

an apron, but for church she had a special dressy dress. She was a widow for 30 years, but she had been married more than 50 years.

When she was about 96 years old, she went to live with Auntie Annie Wilt in Redwood Falls, MN. John

Grandma Mary Kojetin with
Baby Ed Kodet. 1924

48

Wilt, Auntie Annie's husband, had passed away several years before.

She lived with her about two years until Auntie Annie was in a car accident, and couldn't care for her any longer. Then she spent the last years of her life at Sunwood Nursing Home in Redwood Falls, Minnesota.

She died a few days before Dan and Arlene, my son and his wife, were married. The funeral would normally have been on their wedding day, but my parents asked it to be held a day later. So the day after the wedding we went to Grandma's funeral at St. Mary's church in Bechyn. She was buried beside Grandpa in the cemetery by the church.

There was a custom in Bechyn that when anybody died the church bell would toll the age of that person. Hank Schneider was the bell ringer, and he had to ring the bell ninety nine times for Grandma. When you were busy on the farm, and the bell would toll, we would stop what we were doing, and listen to how many times the bell rang for the age of the person who died. If we knew of someone who was sick, we would have an idea of the person identity. One time it rang thirteen times, and we knew that Rose Dolezal had died of leukemia. She was a dear cousin several months younger than me, and God had called her home. We would say a prayer for the person who passed away.

I was five years when my other Grandma, Mary Swoboda Kodet passed away, so I don't remember much about her.

She also always wore long dresses, and an apron. She walked bent over, and had a hard time moving. I remember at Christmas she had a big one hundred pound bag of peanuts behind the door in the parlor, and we all got our own dish of peanuts to eat. Grandpa died before I was born, but Charlie and Ella, Dad's brother and sister, lived with Grandma. Ella could play the pump organ that they had in the parlor. A very beautiful antique organ, I wonder what happened to it.

I remember the funeral in 1934, the driveway to the farm yard was quite long, and not graveled in places. It was raining, and the ground got quite muddy in places. The Model A could get up the driveway, but some of the cars had quite a time. She was buried by Grandpa Wencel Kodet, at the St. Mary's cemetery Bechyn, MN. I don't know how old she was, but I think she was in her 70's. If my numbers are right she would have been seventy four when she died.

When we were in Bohemia, Czechoslovakia, we were in the Bechyne cemetery, and we found graves for Kodet and Swoboda. Curt my son, Deb, my daughter and Tobi, Alphonse's German cousin were able to dig a little soil from each grave that we brought home with us.

Grandma, Mary Swoboda Kodet, Born April 01,1861. Her family settled in Jordan, Mn. And later moved to Renville County. She died May, 1935

I'll always remember my Grandmas with love, and sweet memories.

September 10,1950, Grandma Mary Kojetin's 80th birthday with my Mother, her daughter, Barbara

50

CHAPTER FIFTEEN
Making Hay

· ·

Making hay in the late 1930's, and early 1940's

It was that time of the year. Time to make hay. Our farm had several low spots that weren't plowed, as they filled with water. It was the days before fields were tiled. When the water dried up the prairie grass it would grow thick and tall. This would be the best wild hay for our horses.

Dad would hook the horses to the mower to cut the meadow, but first he'd sharpen the sickle. The round grindstone would be mounted on a wooden frame, and would have bicycle type pedals that would turn the grindstone. There was a half tire under the stone that would be filled with water to keep the stone wet. So each sickle section was sharpened by tilting it this way, and that way. This sickle was only five or six feet long, so it took many rounds to mow the meadow.

After the meadow was mowed, the sun would dry the hay. When it was dry enough Dad would hook the horses to the dump rake. He would rake the hay, and dump it into rows across the field. This made it easier to load onto racks. This hay was going to be put into the big hay barn loft.

There was a track in the top of the hay loft on which slings of hay would travel until a rope was pulled, and they were dumped into the right spot, but first the big door was opened. The big heavy hay barn rope was attached to the door, so it was opened slowly. The big rope went the length of the barn on pulleys in strategic places, and then down, and out to the outside corner to another pulley on a post out there. This is where the horses were hooked to the rope, and as they pulled the rope the slings filled with hay that would go up into the barn. Mother would drive the team, Frank and Bill, and Dad would handle the rope that would trip the sling.

After the hay was dumped we kids were out there to pull the rope back as the horses backed up. The empty sling would come out of the barn, and Dad would hook up the next sling. These slings were placed on the load right in the meadow as the hay was loaded. We had three meadows on our farm, and they were enough to fill the hay barn.

We also had an alfalfa field, but that hay was made into stacks in the field. It was better hay for the cows, and it was hauled in as needed. This was days before balers. This hay was also mowed, and then raked into rows, but instead of loading the hay on racks, Dad would use a bucker. The bucker was a strange looking implement that had a row of long wooden, "teeth" about ten feet long, and a horse would be hooked on each side on a long pole. Dad would walk behind, and go down a row of hay, and fill up the area between the horses, and take it to the stack. Sometimes we were short of help, so I helped on the stack. Mother showed me how to stack the hay- a fork full on the edge another forkful in the middle to tie it in. The idea was so the hay wouldn't slide out, and ruin the stack. She and I would catch the hay, and Emil and Ed would throw it up.
Some farmers had hay loaders or hay stackers. These were machines that would run the hay right up the stacks, so they saved a lot of labor.

It was a beautiful sight to see these haystacks in the fields, and it was a good feeling to the farmers to know they had feed for their livestock.

I watched Dad put the harnesses on the horses many times. They would hang on these big pegs on the barn wall, and they looked very heavy, and also the horse collars. If the harnesses were hung up carefully, there was a trick to place them on the horse correctly. In the summer time there fly nets attached to the harness. The flies were a real pest to the horses, especially the ears. Dad would have a special ointment to put on their ears.

I don't know what happened to the horses, Frank, Bill and the others, on our farm. Alphonse said his Dad traded in their horses on farm machinery.

When I was growing up each farmer would save the best ears of corn from his field for seed the following year. That happened on the Kodet farm also. Some

August, 1945, Emil, his wife, Rosella, whom we all called Babe, Johanna, Barbara, Mother, and Dad

of this corn went on the attic floor, so it dried slowly, and we also put some under the bed in the boy's room. What a chore that was cleaning around that corn. It did not always stay under the bed, so we would stack it up from time to time. That helped keep the room neat. I'm so surprised that we didn't have mice. They would have loved that.

In the spring the corn was shelled with a hand sheller, and used for seed. When hybrid corn was discovered, it produced so much better that farmers did not save their own seed anymore.

Soybeans was a crop that was not produced in Minnesota at

that time. When we were first married it was just beginning to be used as a crop especially in low places.

Making Hay, Johanna, Mother, Dad and Emil

53

CHAPTER SIXTEEN
Chimney Fire

· ·

It was a late fall day, the trees had lost their leaves. The days were beginning to get cold, and the nights even colder.

I was about eight or nine years old. I was upstairs in my room trying on my new dress. Mother and Dad had been shopping, and I loved my new dress. Someone kept calling me, "supper is ready, come and eat!!!!" BUT I POKED ALONG, admiring how I looked in the mirror. Then I heard- "FIRE!! FIRE!! COME QUICK!!!!!!!" I ran down stairs, and I did not take my new dress off.

It was a chimney fire. We were all outside, flames were coming out of the chimney.

We had all been in the house having supper-until the neighbors started driving in. They had seen the fire through the trees. Our angels, Uncle John Wilt, and Uncle Wencel Kojetin were there, and also others. They got the tall ladder to the top of the roof, and Uncle Wencel went up the ladder, and threw chemicals in the fire,

July 18,1946, Barbara and Martha by the fence Mother wanted. Note the ladder on the roof on the right.

they were just chemicals. He got up on the roof, and he started throwing small boxes or balls or something trying to land them in the chimney. I guess it worked because the fire went down, and went out.

After it cooled off, they put a small ladder on the roof to reach the chimney. They tied a rope on a log chain, and the chain went into the chimney to knock the soot off the walls. There was a clean out door way at the bottom of the chimney in the basement. They cleaned all the soot, and junk out of the chimney. That had to be quite a job to drag that heavy log chain up the big ladder, and the smaller ladder on the roof.

After that Dad had a special ladder that stayed on the roof, so they could clean the chimney a couple times a year. All the wood and cobs in the cook stove, and wood and coal in the furnace caused the soot to catch on the walls of the chimney. Later on my sister, Martha, told me it was salt that was thrown into the burning chimney.

We kids sat in the Model A Ford, and watched the fire, as they were putting it out. We were praying our house would not burn down, but I was sure glad I was wearing my new dress.

Mother and Dad used to entertain a lot, especially in the winter. So that was a good reason to have a party, to thank those who helped put out the fire. We kids would be sent to bed after a while, but we would peek down through the register in our room. We soon got tired of that, and got into bed, and went to sleep.

October 29,1918. Wedding picture of Alois E. Kodet and Barbara Kojetin, my parents.

55

CHAPTER SEVENTEEN
Grocery Shopping

· ·

I remember when there were no carts in grocery stores. A lot of products came in bulk displays- such as a barrel of, "pickles" or kegs of sugar, brown sugar, cereals, rice, raisins among other things.

Mother would make a list. We had so much of our own food on the farm, but there were other things we'd need. We would drive to Olivia on Friday night or Saturday afternoon, and make it a gay occasion.

While we went to the movie, Mother took her list to the Halliday grocery store. Uncle George and Aunt Emma were the owners. In the back of the store they would take in eggs, cream, poultry, fur pelts, etc. Aunt Emma would take the list, and start packaging bulk products that Mother needed. A pound of this, two pounds of that. She would weigh the amount – put it in a brown paper bag, and tie it with a string. The string came in a huge cone, and it was hung in a special hanger above the counter, hanging down. She'd fold the bag down, and tie a

1953, L-R: My cousins Susan, Betty, Aunt Emma Kojetin Halliday, Sister Emma George and Angela Kojetin Frank. Susan and Betty are Angela's daughters, and Sister is Emma's daughter.

couple rounds of string around it, and place it in a box. She had a keen eye for judging the size of the box by the size of the list. Sometimes more than one box, there seemed to be a big supply of boxes, all sizes. Many customers would save the string, and add on to the ball of string at home. The string came in handy for many things.

Flour and sugar also came in hundred pound bags, salt also in fifty pound bags. Oatmeal was always on the list, Dad had oatmeal every morning for breakfast. Rock candy also, it was a favorite, and chocolate candy was a huge treat.

There was some fruit and veggies available, but if anyone had an extra supply, they were glad to sell it. Mother took her strawberries and raspberries to the grocery store already displayed in small boxes to be sold. Hallidays grocery was happy to buy them.

We kids would go to the movie. For a dime admission we would see a double feature. Mostly cowboy shows – Gene Autry, Roy Rogers, Tom Mix, Hopalong Cassidy, were some of them. Also the Lone Ranger, Tonto and many others. The good guys always wore the white hats. The theater would be full. Saturday night was always, "bank night." Ticket stubs had a number, and if you were lucky you might win a cash prize. Five dollars was a big prize, many one dollar prizes.

The women were given a piece of, "depression glass." Mother had a set of these beautiful glass dishes in pink. They also came in bags of flour, and certain products. Some depression glass was green or gold also.

The Sleepy Eye Flour Mill gave out, "Chief Sleepy Eye," pitchers, sugar bowls, cups, and glasses in their bags of flour. They are very scarce, and valuable collector items today.

Bechyn used to have free movies at one time. A big screen was set up not far from Grandpa and Grandma Kojetin's house. I remember one of the movies that was shown. It was about zombies. It was so scary I think I had some scary dreams after that. That's why I remember it. To think Zombies

are back again this day and age. BACK TO GROCERY
SHOPPING!!!!!!!!!!!!!!!!!

Carts in grocery stores started being used a few years after
Alphonse and I were married. I believe Jenkins in New Ulm was
the first store to use them – a predecessor of HyVee.

We, Alphonse and I, used to shop in Morton at the Mercantile
which was a general store, it had clothing, dry goods and
groceries, and at Al Heineke's grocery, locker and frozen food
storage. Jim Ryan's grocery came in after the Mercantile closed.
Morton used to be a bustling town with a hardware store, drug
store, bank, shoe store, doctor, (Dr. Lenz), lawyer, barber,
plumber, carpenters, three restaurants, liquor store, four gas
stations, auto mechanics, hatchery, bakery, the big hotel by the
railroad track that was also another restaurant, blacksmith, grain
elevator, feed stores, Morton granite quarry, lumber yard, city
hall which doubled as a center for weddings, and events, three
churches, and of course the school. We had wonderful teachers
that taught a lot of smart kids. I can't forget the farmers that
lived in the area and supported the town.

Alphonse and I had settled on a farm four miles south of
Morton close to where Jackpot Junction Casino is today, just
south of the Indian Reservation. We lived on this farm for
twenty years from 1946 to 1966 when we moved with our fifteen
children to a farm by
Sleep Eye.

September 10,1950,
L-R: The Kojetin children
and their spouses, Mother
and Dad, Emma and George
Halliday, Josephine and
Henry F. Frank, Anna and,
John, Grandma Mary Kojetin,
Mary Kodet, (John Kodet
deceased brother of
my Dad,) Jennie and Jim
Wertish, Angela and Henry P.
Frank and Wencel and Katie
Kojetin.

CHAPTER EIGHTTEEN
Bechyn Celebrations

· ·

Every year in June, St. Mary's Catholic Church in Bechyn would have a big celebration to honor Corpus Christi, (Body of Christ.) There would be a high mass- all the First Communion girls would dress in their white dresses, and veils, and the boys in their white shirts and ties. There would be a procession that would go out on the church grounds to three altars that were prepared to receive the Blessed Sacrament. It was led by an altar boy carrying a processional cross.

The altars were a framework put up by the men, and decorated by the young women in the, "Young Ladies Sodality". Martha and I were in a group of four that decorated one altar. We would use white sheets to cover the arch shaped frame. (There was no such thing as colored or printed sheets.) We would trim with white lace, and lots of flowers. There was a small table that we covered with white tablecloth, and lace also. We placed two candles, and a crucifix on the table, and two vases of fresh flowers. On the ground we placed a scatter rug. Mother always had lots of flowers, and June was a month of many blooming perennials.

There was a competition among the three groups who could make their altar the most beautiful. As the procession went along, one of the men would go ahead, and light the candles. The people would follow the children, and then the choir would come, the altar boys, and then the priest carried the Blessed

Sacrament. He was walking under a fringed canopy carried by four men. Martha and I belonged to the choir, and we would sing for Benediction at each altar. Later a big dinner was held for all in the church basement.

It was so beautiful, the lawn was freshly mowed, and flower beds in full bloom. My sister, Lydia and her husband, Joe, were there with their two little girls, Barbara and Jean. Brother Emil and wife Rosella, (Babe), with son Dick, and baby daughter, Diane were also there. The summer after Alphonse and I were married, we went back for the celebration. It was a hot day, and the sun was shining down. We were standing, and kneeling among the crowd. I told Alphonse, "I didn't feel well," He put his arm around me just before I fainted. Next thing I remember he was carrying me, (no he didn't sling me over his shoulder,) in the parking lot. My Mother was sitting in the car with Granddaughter, Barbara, as she had been fussy. Mother said, "Bring her over here," so Alphonse took me over to be by Mother. Her car was in the shade in the line of trees. By that time I had woken up, and the cool air felt good. I was three months pregnant, and the heat did not agree with me. Later, in December, Linda was born, but that's another story, a very good story. I was able to join everyone for the meal in the church basement, and the fun and games later.

There were picnic tables set up under the huge cottonwood trees, and the young men were playing baseball against the neighboring town team. The cemetery is close to the church, and it too had been just mowed, and decorated with flowers.

June 22,1946 LR: Barbara, Martha, Angie Serbus and Martha Frank, Corpus Christie celebration.

They, also sponsored a bazaar later in the year- also

held outdoors. A dinner would be served, and many games for the kids, and bingo for the adults.

1879 - 1992

St. Mary's Catholic Church, Bechyn, Minnesota

CHAPTER NINETEEN
Relatives on the Kodet Side

· ·

I was asked to write an article on your cousins on the Kodet side of the family. Many of you don't know all your relatives. There are many so you'll never know all of them.

Dad had four brothers, and five sisters. John was oldest in the family, and he married Mary Kojetin, (Mother's oldest sister.) They raised nine children, six boys and three girls, Matilda, Mary and Philothea. The only girls surviving are Mary Knaesbero, Renville, Minnesota, and Philothea of Minneapolis, Minnesota. The boys are Roman, Stanley, Ray, Edmund, John (Jack) and Wencel. They all ended up in the cities. I don't know if any served in the military. Their farm was just south of the country school.

Dad's sister Anna and Mary were the oldest girls, and they married brothers, Anna and John Zetah, and Frank and Mary Zetah. They settled on farms about four miles north of us. John and Anna had ten children, five boys and five girls. Ben, Alvin, Alois and Richard were all in the military, army and navy. Hattie married Ed Herdina, Bernice Married George Houdek, Margie married Bernard Fesemaier who still lives in Olivia, and Ellen is married and lives in the cities.

Frank and Mary Zetah had 13 children, seven boy and six girls, Ray, Vern, Frank, Leonard all served in the military. Joe, Jerry and Jim were identical triplets, couldn't tell them apart. You called one name-they would all look. Two of the girls,

Doris and Muriel became nuns in California. Alice married Stan Nester from Renville, Minnesota, Mary and Theresa were the same ages of Adella and I, but all the family is deceased except Jerry and Joe.

Emma married Wencel, (James) Dolezal, they had thirteen children, ten boys and three girls. Alois, Ed, Leo, Joe, Harry, Frank, Charley, Leonard, all served in the military, army and navy, except Miloyd and John who were too young. Joe lived in the Foley area so we probably have relatives there.

Buddy, (Miloyd) settled on the home farm near North Redwood. Most of the boys are deceased except Buddy and possible Charley who lives in California. Magdalen married Laurence Lundstrom- the family who stared the Lundstrom musical group. Mary and Rose Marie- Mary lived in Oregon after marriage, and Rose Marie died of leukemia at the age of thirteen. She could play anything on the piano. The girls are all deceased. Emma passed away at the age of 66 years. Later Wencel married Louise who had been married to Joe Kodet, (Dad's brother). He had passed away so Wencel and Louise were married. Dad was the fifth child born to Wencel and Mary Kodet. Next were Joe and Adolph, and they married sisters. Joe married Louise Senkyr, and Adolph married Ludmila Senkyr. Joe and Louise had four boys and one girl. Angeline, She married Ben Kahout, and still lives in Olivia, Minnesota, and is in her nineties. Elmer, Leonard, Otto and Bonitus, (Bonnie), were all in the military in World War II, army and navy. Elmer and Leonard Kodet married sisters, Mary and Betty Malecek. You probably know some of their children. Elmer and Mary's children are Galen, Donald, Dennis, Elaine, Phyllis, (married Stan Abbas and lives in Arizona as does Elaine,) and Betty married Dan Bennett. Elmer and Mary lived on the home farm, and are both deceased.

Leonard and Betty settled in North Redwood, Minnesota. They have three children, Carolyn Kissel of Yankton, South Dakota, Allan, (Diane,) Kodet lives in Paynesville, Minnesota, and Robert, (Louise) live in Northfield, Minnesota. I don't know too much about Otto and Bonnie Kodet, but I do know Otto passed away. His son Gary farms near Morgan, Minnesota.

Dad's brother Charley never married, and he worked for a dairy farmer near New Prague, Minnesota, for many years. Dad's sister, Ella, also never married, and lived on the home farm until she died. Our brother, Alois Jr., was her care giver, and he always checked on her, and brought groceries for her.

Katherine married Joe Dworshak. They lived south of Bechyn about four miles. They had three children, Bernard, MaryAnn and Katherine. Bernard lived on the home farm in later years.

We use to go and visit all these families, usually on a Sunday afternoon. All the boys who served their country in World War II came home, my brother, Ed came back, and my youngest brother, Alois Jr., was too young at the time, but he was in the National Guard for eight years.

CHAPTER TWENTY
Relatives on the Kojetin Side

My Mother had six sisters, and one brother. Anna married John Wilt, and they had an adopted son, Joe, who passed away at age 22. They were Godparents for all of us nine children.

Mary married John Kodet, Dad's brother, and they were written up in the story of the Kodet Side.

Josephine married Henry F. Frank, and they farmed east of us about four miles. They had five boys and three girls. Bill, Milo, Wencel, Henry Jr. and Bernard. They were all farmers except for Milo, who had a gas station, and a gas truck out of Olivia, Minnesota. Henry married Mary Jane Herdina, and Bernard married JoAnn Keaveny. Henry is retired, and now lives in Willmar, Minnesota, and Bernard is on the home farm. Angela Married Francis Elbert, and she passed away. Rita married Robert Hilgert, and Sylvia married Elfering. Both live near Bird Island, Minnesota. Franks had Beaver Creek running through their property, and when we'd visit, us kids always went by the creek. Emma married George Halliday, and they had a grocery store in Olivia, Minnesota. George was also a carpenter, and helped build the new Bechyn church, St. Marys. They had four sons and four daughters. Leo, Ray, Cyril and George Jr. (Junky.) All served in the World War II, and all returned. Junky was badly wounded, and two of them were POWs. Four daughters, Adella, Mary Ann, Helen and Barbara. Adella married, and lived in Washington. She passed away last year. Mary Ann lives in

Olivia, Minnesota, and was a teacher in Catholic schools, and is now retired. Helen is in a care center in Minneapolis, Minnesota, after suffering a stroke, near her daughter, and Barbara lives in Texas. Angela married Henry P. Frank, and they lived N.W. of Bechyn about six miles. They had two sons Myron and Donald, both farmers now retired. Myron married Elaine Mages, (Alphonse's sister,) and they had ten children- two boys and eight girls. Darwin, Tony, Kathy, Theresa, Connie, Beverly, Mary, Christine, Joan and Brenda. Donald married Veronica Serbus.

Henrietta married Clarence Mages, (Alphonse's brother,) and they had eight children, five boys and three girls, Jerome, Raymond, David, Donald, and Randy, and girls Marie, Judy and Doreen. Clarence and Henrietta were farmers now retired. Henrietta is deceased and Clarence lives in Willmar, Minnesota. Johanna, (Jennie,) was married to Jim Wertish, and they lived on a farm two miles east of Olivia. They had ten children—I know the names of Martha, Leo and Cyril-the older ones. Martha married Rene Macek from Bird Island, Minnesota. When we used to visit them, we would play cricket, an outdoor game something like baseball. Martha's husband passed away, and she now lives in Hector, Minnesota. Cy had a hog farm north of Hector, Minnesota, about four or five miles.

Wencel married Catherine Kodet, and lived on the home farm just south of where we lived. They had two sons, Wencel Jr. and John, and two daughters, Regina and Mary Jane. Wencel Jr. and his wife Carol live along Highway 71 halfway between Morton and Olivia, Minnesota. John and his wife Marie Malecek lived in Willmar, Minnesota, before he died. Regina lives with her husband, Ellsworth Pockrandt in Gibbon, Minnesota. They

1940, Mary Lou, cousin Henrietta Frank, Angela Kojetin Frank's daughter and Adella

66

used to manage the Gibbon Ballroom for many years. Mary Jane married John Nordby. Uncle Wencel and Aunt Katy lived well into their nineties, and they both passed to their heavenly home in the same week, a few days apart.

Emma
&
Barbara
April 1918

1918, Emma Kojetin, (Halliday,) and Barbara Kojetin, (Kodet,) my mother.
Sorry for the distorted photo,
but thought it was still an important photo to use in this book.

CHAPTER TWENTY ONE
Boy Meets Girl

. . . .

It was April in 1944, it was a very rainy month, and if a road didn't have enough gravel on it, it was very muddy. There was going to be a wedding at St. Mary's in Bechyn. My sister, Martha, and I sang in the choir, and we are going to sing at the wedding.

Annie Kozubik is getting married to Alphonse's Uncle, Henry Zins from Wabasso, Minnesota. The sun is out today for the wedding day- how lovely.

There are many strangers in church, as the groom is from a large family. We notice three young men especially. They are not groomsmen, but some of the relatives of Henry. We have a good view from the choir loft, so we keep our eyes on them, anyway I do.

We are not invited to the reception, but we did plan on going to the wedding dance that night at the Morton City Hall in Morton, Minnesota. Martha and I went with my brother Ed, my sister, Lydia and husband Joe were married, and they were at the dance also, as were many of our friends.

Dances were different at that time. The band started playing at nine pm, and played until 1 am. There was a half hour intermission at 11:30 pm. There were no tables, or chairs in the dance hall. There were benches along the side, but mostly people stood in groups.

I was standing with my friends when this young man came,

and asked me to dance. I recognized him as being in church that morning. His name was Alphonse Mages. I told him my name was Barbara Kodet. We had a nice dance. Alphonse was dressed in a suit, white shirt, and pretty yellow tie.

The next dance Alphonse asked me again, and again. At the third dance he asked me if I'd go to intermission with him. I said I didn't know for sure, but I would ask my sister, Lydia. It seems my brother, Ed, and sister, Lydia were keeping an eye on me. Lydia and Joe said it would be okay, if we'd all go together. So the next dance I told Alphonse yes, if he'd meet my family.

Now at intermission the band would take a break, and most people would leave the dance, and walk uptown to a restaurant, and have a soda or ice cream or some refreshment. At intermission Lydia and Joe went with Alphonse and me, so they asked him a lot of questions. He was from a farm near Morgan, Minnesota, and the groom was his Uncle.

After intermission we danced again, but he did not ask to take me home. At least I didn't have to refuse Alphonse as Lydia told me it would not be a good idea if he asked to take me home. He was going to join his brother, Albin and Uncle LeRoy Zins.

I had fun that night, and really enjoyed the dance.

I found out later that Alphonse, his brother, Albin, and Uncle LeRoy had a plan that each one would take out a girl for intermission, or be called a, "sad sack. Albin had taken out Rita Kodet, and LeRoy had taken Sally Kodet for intermission. So the following Sunday they came to Bechyn looking for the Kodet girls. (Sally and Rita were second cousins to me.) They found Sally at home, but her Dad said, "No Sally can't go to the movies with you." Same way with Rita, who was also my neighbor. Her Dad said no, she can't go to the movies.

But they didn't find me. They were in my neighborhood, but they didn't find me.

We said if three young men came on our yard like that, Dad would have probably invited them to play horseshoe.

But Alphonse did not give up. Later that summer Alphonse

and brother, Albin found out that Bechyn had dances every Sunday night, so they came to a dance. My brother, Ed recognized him, and asked if he was looking for Barbara? He said, "Yes. " I guess he thought he was really in luck.

Ed said that Uncle John and Aunt Anna Wilt were having a party, and she is probably there at the party. So they went to Wilts. All the men were in the basement having a beer, so they stayed to visit for a while. But no Barbara at the party, so Ed showed Alphonse where I lived, but no one home there either.

But, Ed did tell him that I was staying in the nearby town of Olivia, Minnesota, at my Uncle and Aunt, George and Emma Halliday during the school year, but I was home on weekends. He told Alphonse where their house was in Olivia.

One night there was a knock on the front door. Aunt Emma answered the door, and there was Alphonse. Aunt Emma called me, and I went downstairs, and I was surprised to see him. I hadn't seen him since the wedding dance. Alphonse wanted to take me to a dance in Renville,

Alphonse and Barbara at a waterfall in the Black Hills in South Dakota

Minnesota, another close town. Aunt Emma recognized Alphonse from the night of the Wilts party. Uncle George wasn't home, but Aunt Emma told Alphonse it was a school night, and, "don't keep Barbara out too late."

Alphonse waited in the living room while I got ready. I had no "Sunday clothes" along, only school clothes, but cousin Adella got one of her dresses, "I think this will fit you," she said. It was a beautiful red dress. Adella helped me get ready, meanwhile cousins, Mary Ann, Helen and Barbara were peeking into the living room from time to time. I really got teased later.

We went to the dance, and had a very good time getting to

know each other. We made a date to see each other to go to a wedding dance in Morgan, Minnesota, about two weeks later. His Aunt Agnes, who had lost her husband, Bernard Mages, was getting married again.

When we were celebrating our 50th wedding anniversary, Alphonse told me that he still remembered the dress I was wearing when he met me the first time. So I had to test his memory. Yes, I was wearing a two piece green dress. The skirt was plain green, but the top was kind of striped, and fitted just right.

Alphonse and Barbara

CHAPTER TWENTY TWO
Bits and Pieces

. . . .

Someone asked me to write more about the horses we had on the farm when I was growing up.

There were the white horses, Bill and Frank. I think they were Dad's favorite team. They were the first ones that were harnessed, and hitched up to a field implement or hay rack, or the sleigh in the winter time. All our horses were big horses, not as big as the Percherons or Clydesdales, but I guess you could call them draft horses.

Then there were Fanny, Jess and Tom. When Ed and I would take a team at corn picking time we would use any two of these. They would all work well together.

Fanny and Tom were a dark brown color, and Jess had a brownish red color. Tom was a favorite of us kids because we could ride him. We all had our turn riding bareback. We didn't have a saddle. Tom had his bridle on most of the time, but he would need the bit in his mouth, and the reins were attached to that. Whichever way you pulled on the reins he would turn that way. If you wanted to stop you would say, "Whoa," and pull back on the reins. Of course, you would coax him to go by jiggling the reins and saying, "Giddiap." We would ride him up and down the field road, and out to the meadows.

Mary Lou, my younger sister, tells the story of her and Junior riding the horse. My little brother was, "Junior," all his growing up years. When we were adults we called him Al, (Alois Kodet

Jr.) Anyway, Junior wanted her to go riding with him. She said, "If you let me ride in the saddle," (later on they had a saddle for Tom,) so they agreed to that. Junior sat behind her, and they had a nice ride around the farm. They were coming back on the field road when a mosquito landed on her arm. Mary Lou swatted it with a loud smack, and Tom bolted so fast, Junior went right off the horse's tail, and landed in the dirt. The horse, Tom, ran so fast, but Mary Lou was able to slow him down before they got to the barn. They had a big laugh about it later as long as no one got hurt.

Junior had a lot of good times riding Tom. When he was still very young he'd ride bare back, or way back on the horse. He'd walk on his back, and Tom put up with all his acrobatics.

I have a story about Jess also. She was out in the yard that was shared with the cattle. The bull did not take a liking to her that day, and he started to attack her. Then he would run around the other side of the barn, and come with greater speed, and run into her, almost knocking her over. Dad happened to notice this, and he ran to the barn, and quickly opened the door, and got Jess inside before the bull came again. Here the bull came running again, but Jess was already safe in the barn.

Mother could handle the teams very well. She could drive them over when they were in harness, and one horse would step over the pole. She'd back up the team a little, and they wait to be hitched to the trailer, or hay rack or whatever. Then she would hook up the traces, or tugs to the eveners. Then she would lift the pole in front, and attach that to the harnesses. Ready to go!!!!

I should write a little about the, "front porch" on our house where I grew up. Now you would probably call it a three season room. It had a hardwood floor like the rest of the floors downstairs except the kitchen. It had many windows, and was on the east side of the house, so the afternoon sun did not heat it. We spent many summer evenings out there. On one side was the sewing machine, and Mother's wooden rocker with the leather seat. We all took our turns learning to sew. The first thing we learned was hemming dish towels. It had to be done neatly, and evenly. We used much flour, and sugar which came in bags. We would open the seams, and bleach them, and they made excellent dish towels. We would embroider a picture in the corner, and after doing a set of six or seven they went into our, "hope chest." Each one of us girls had a cedar chest in which we would put special things that would help set up a household someday. We would generally get a cedar chest on our sixteenth birthday, and we already had something to put into it.

On the other side of the room was a daybed, and some chairs. Now this was not an ordinary daybed. It was a soft bed with no back or sides, but it had big pillows. It was a perfect place to snuggle up with a good book for a rainy afternoon, or just for a quiet time. Mother would be sitting in her rocker saying a rosary, I think praying for Ed, and so he would come home safely from the army. Sometimes I would join her.

It was a great place to sit in the evening, and watch for the car that was bringing your date. We teased Albin,(Alphonse's brother,) and Alphonse that we could all ready see them coming from Highway 71, because of all the dust they were raising. That was almost three miles away.

We did a lot of shopping in Redwood Falls, MN. There were many good stores, Ehlers and Galles come to my mind because if we needed a new dress or coat, we shopped there. This particular day we were walking past Galles, and stopped to window shop. There was one dress that caught our eye, it was so pretty. Mother had a brilliant idea that she could make them. We went next door to Silverbergs. It was a store that sold mostly household products, but also yard material. We picked out material to make four dresses, for Martha, Adella, Mary Lou and Me. We bought matching thread and big buttons. Mother made her own pattern. Martha and I wore the same size but Adella and Mary Lou were also different sizes. She sewed that week, and by Sunday we wore our new dresses to church. It was a sleeveless dress with a square neckline, with buttons all the way down the front. The belt was set in with a slightly flared skirt. One dress was kind of dusty blue, one a dusty green, and one a dusty gold. Mary Lou's was a print in white, red and yellow. She had made all the buttonholes by hand which was a big job. We loved those dresses, and wore them often that summer.

I have to write about my first driving experience. It was with our Model A Ford. We kids learned how to clutch, and shift the gears as soon as our legs were long enough to reach the pedals. My Dad would leave the car parked in front of the garage after church. We would take turns shifting and clutching- reverse-clutch-low-clutch-second-clutch- high. It didn't hurt the car when the motor was off. This one spring day, I was probably 12 or 13 years old, somebody had to take lunch out to Dad and Mother. They're putting in small grain on the twenty acres on the other side of the ditch. The short cut through the pasture was blocked as the ditch that ran through the pasture was full of water. Have to go on the road. I decided to take the car. I backed it out of the garage, and started out. But the steering was so tricky. I was wobbling all over the driveway. OK, steady now. When Dad drives he holds the wheel pretty steady. I'm getting the hang of it. No cars are coming, so I get on the road, but the scary part is coming.

Up ahead the road ditches are on both sides of the road, and are full of water, Steady now- I make it through. Whew!!!!!! Dad and Mother see me

January 1946, Dad with the horses Bill and Frank.

coming. WHO THE HECK IS DRIVING THE CAR?   They
happened to be at the end of the field, filling up the drill with
seed. I get out of the car and say, "I've got lunch. I've got
coffee." They ask me a lot of questions, and then Dad says, "Go
to the corner, and turn around, and take it home." This time
the road between the water was not quite as scary. I parked the
car in front of the garage. I wasn't going to chance on banging
up the garage door. When I was fifteen Mother took me to the
courthouse in Olivia, MN. I got my driver's license, no written
test, no driving test. It cost fifty cents.

CHAPTER TWENTY THREE
The Dating Years

· ·

We didn't have a telephone, and neither did the Mages' have a phone. At first Alphonse would come on Sunday afternoon, and wonder if I would like to see a movie. Then we'd make a date for the following week-end. Albin would come along, and Adella would go to the movie too. Martha was engaged to Clarence Serbus, but after D-Day he left for the army. In the fall Albin also went into basic training, so my sister Adella wrote letters, and Martha wrote to Clarence.

Alphonse and Albin had an Uncle, LeRoy Zins that was just a few years older than they were. LeRoy was dating a Bechyn girl, Theresa Houdek, so we'd all get together, and have picnics etc. LeRoy had a maroon car that a speck of dust didn't dare to land on it. LeRoy also had leukemia. He would have to get a blood transfusion at a hospital in Minneapolis every month. Either Alphonse or Albin would travel with him, and sometimes they stayed overnight. There wasn't any such thing as chemo treatments at that time. LeRoy also was a serious guy, but he loved humor, and he would pull tricks on his nephews. He worked at Montgomery Wards in Redwood Fall, Minnesota, down in the hardware area, and also the shoe department. Now Montgomery Wards was a big store- had three levels full of merchandise. It was next to the Redwood Theater which also was a big building with a balcony upstairs. It had a carpeted lounge with fancy chairs, and restrooms before you went into the balcony. Also a crying room up there as many parents brought children to the movie.

Redwood Falls had another new theater called the Falls Theater. It had no balcony, but it had a fancy lounge, and restrooms on the lower level. Both theaters were always well attended. We saw many movies, and afterward we would go, and have ice cream.

On Sunday night we went to Bechyn dances, or later on to the Gibbon Ballroom at Gibbon, Minnesota, or wedding dances in other towns. Every town had a dance hall, there were even some barn dances.

When Clarence Serbus, Ed Kodet, my brother, and Albin went into the army we got together more with Clarence's sisters Cele and Marie, and their boyfriends Harlan B. and Harry S. Harlan wanted to know if we ever saw the Minnesota capital building, so we all planned a picnic, and drove to the cities. My first time I was amazed at the tall buildings. To think at that time, the Foshay Tower was the tallest building. Alphonse knew his way around because of his trips with LeRoy.

But sadly, LeRoy had passed away. He was only 22 years old. He was Grandma Elizabeth Mages', brother. Alphonse's family had contacted the Red Cross, if Albin could come home for the funeral, but it wasn't possible. He did come home later on furlough before he went to Europe to join army forces there.

I remember the first time Alphonse took me home to visit his family. His Uncle, Bill Zins, also Grandma Elizabeth's brother, was home on furlough after being in the Aleutian Islands, Alaska for several years. Alphonse's Dad and Mom were putting on a party for the Zins family, so I met many people. Theresa Houdek was also there, so I had somebody I knew. They were all so friendly, and they teased Alphonse, so they made me laugh. I met his brother, Ozzie, who was in a wheelchair, and his brother, Clarence, and sisters, Elaine and Diane. Bill looked like an older LeRoy. He was going to use LeRoy's car, but he was going back to serve in Europe first.

TO BECHYN AND BACK

During Lent, we didn't go to dances or movies, but every Sunday night we had a house party. We'd play games or cards. If there was a piano we'd sing songs as Marie or Cele played the piano. Cele played the organ in church as we sang in the choir. Marie played by ear, so she could play anything. I remember one party at our house when we got my Dad involved in playing games-Ring on a String. Put a ring on a heavy cord, and tie the ends together. Everyone sits in the circle, and passes the ring while "IT" stands in the middle of the circle, and tries to guess where the ring is. Always had a good lunch.

When Lent was over we planned to go to dance at the Gibbon Ballroom, so we told Alphonse we'd pick him up as he was, "on the way." We drove on his yard with two cars, and picked him up. We had much fun dancing to the "old time," music.

Alphonse asked if Adella, and I would like to help his mother shell peas for canning, so I said, "Yes we'd love to." One June morning he came, and picked us up about 8 am, and we drove back home with him. She already had the peas picked. What a crop, many pails of peas, so we got to work shelling those peas. I'm sure we ate a few as we filled the bowls. We had a good time visiting, and eating some of her good cooking. Alphonse's sister Elaine helped also, and sister Diane was so sweet. Alphonse took us home later that day after he did his milking chores.

Sometimes on a Sunday night our group would stop at the Mages' south of the Minnesota River, and pick Alphonse up for the dance at the Gibbon Ballroom.

There was one time though when Martha, Adella and I went with Alphonse to a dance at the New Ulm Ballroom in New Ulm, Minnesota. Whoopee John Band was playing music, and he played at Alphonse's folks wedding dance. The New Ulm Ballroom was located in the area where Kraft is today. When it closed it was taken over by Goodrich Tires. It was a long way to go, fifty miles from our place by Bechyn. We had a great time at the dance, and there were two young men that were flirting with Martha and Adella. They danced with them, and they hung around. Later when intermission came they asked to come along, and so Alphonse said, "Sure." Martha and Adella were already in the back seat of the car, and when they saw them coming, over the seat they went, so we were four in the front seat. We had to drive back to downtown as there were no fast food or Perkins in the area. That part of New Ulm was not developed yet. So Pete and Joe ordered buffalo sandwiches, and gooseberry pie, so we'd had a good time with them. We all ended up with a dish of ice cream. We went back to the dance, and never saw those two young men again. We always teased Martha and Adella about going over the seat.

When we had our prom at the Morton school, it was a closed prom, no outside dates. We had it in the shop at the Morton High School. It was a big room, the big tools were taken out, and it was decorated very pretty. Dad took me, and dropped me off. About 11pm, here comes Alphonse, all dressed up in a suit, (he looked very handsome.) He wanted to join in for just one dance, but the superintendent and principle were both by the door, and they said, "NO." He asked if he could take me home later, but I said my Dad was coming to pick me up. I guess if we'd have telephones we would have had that all settled ahead of time.

We did break up a couple of times. I can't remember the reasons, but I guess it wasn't anything important. He sent me a letter, and said he missed me, and he was coming to pick me up on Saturday night. If I didn't write back, he would come. I guess I missed him too, as I didn't write back.

Alphonse's parents had a 37 Chevrolet, and that was the family car. He got to use the car when his parents weren't using it. You couldn't buy a car-new or used- when the war was on,

Alphonse and Barbara in Montana

so that car got a lot of miles. Later on they were able to pick up a used Ford car for Alphonse in Mankato. That also had a lot of miles on it, but it had a radio!!!!!!!!!!!!!

Alphonse and Barbara in front of his parents home
at rural Morgan, Minnesota

CHAPTER TWENTY FOUR
The Dating Years

. . . .

Alphonse and I went to many movies. Adella and Martha generally went along, unless we were with the bigger group. We liked to go to Ramsey Park in Redwood Falls, and walk the trails and see the Falls.

We enjoyed his car, and he was so proud of it, always kept it very clean. We'd always like to listen to country music on the radio.

The year I was sixteen he gave me a watch for my birthday. First watch I ever had. When I was seventeen he gave me a heart locket, and bracelet set which I still have. We used to take a lot of pictures, so it didn't take long I had our pictures in the locket.

One winter after we had a big blizzard, and the roads were all closed, we saw these lights coming up the driveway. My Dad had the horses, and sleigh out that day bringing some hay from the hay stack, so there were tracks on the driveway. Who is that coming over? It was Alphonse!!! He just about got stuck coming into the yard, but he made it. He had tried three different routes trying to find a road open enough, so he could get through to our place. We went to Redwood Falls to the movies. My Dad said he'd help us get out of the yard, so he pushed, and then hopped on the bumper of the car to put some weight on the back. We didn't know he did that until later he told us. He teased Alphonse the next time he came over that he almost went to the movies with us.

Adella and I were going to Morton High School, so we were always busy doing homework on school nights, so I'd see Alphonse on weekends, but in the summertime we got together a little more often. Although summertime was harvest time. Alphonse was busy on his Dad's farm also with shocking grain and threshing. When he'd come, he and Dad would always have conversations about farming.

Wednesday night was choir practice night, so Alphonse knew where we were, and he'd come there and listen, and later we'd probably go to a movie. It was 1946, but Alphonse's brother Albin, and my future brother in law Clarence Serbus were still in the army. Albin later married Adella and Clarence married Martha.

August 02, 1946. This special Friday night Alphonse didn't come until 9 p.m. We had been threshing oats at my brother Emil's that day, and he also had been threshing at their farm

We, just us two, went to the movie in Redwood Falls called, "As the Walls Came Tumbling Down..." We went, and had an ice cream sundae afterward at Cheney's Cafe. Gennie Zins, Alphonse's Aunt, was a waitress there. Later when he took me home, he asked me to marry him, and, "I SAID YES." He gave me a beautiful diamond ring. We didn't make any wedding plans, just happy to be engaged.

BUT, I had one more year of school to finish. I was a senior, and planned on graduating. BUT, Alphonse's Dad had bought the neighbor's farm. Jens Miller had been a widower for about 15 years, and was living alone on the farm. He was elderly, and not able to attend to all the farm work, so the living place was much neglected. After his harvest was done, Alphonse started plowing there. He was discouraged with all the rocks, the plow kept unhooking when he hit a rock, and he'd have to hook it up again, and again, and again.

Alphonse's Dad, Oswald, and Mother, Elizabeth, wanted us to get married right away, so we could live there. Jens was going to have an auction sale. I kept saying, "not until next

June," BUT, Alphonse had a lot of patience with me, and I finally was persuaded to get married, so we picked the twenty eighth wedding anniversary of my parents, as our wedding date. October 29, 1946.

Now I was going to live south of the river. What a coincidence that the Morton School bus would drive past our home every day. Some of my classmates would now be my neighbors.

Some of the men at Bechyn would talk to my Dad, and say he shouldn't let those Morgan guys come, and take our girls away, but that was just the beginning. My sister, Adella married Albin Mages, Alphonse's sister, Elaine and brother, Clarence Mages married into Bechyn families. Alphonse's cousins dated Bechyn girls, and Eugene Tauer married a Serbus girl from Bechyn.

We had a wedding coming up!!! The reception would be here at home, so we did some painting walls, and housecleaning the house from top to bottom. My Dad and the boys took care of the outside. But the livestock still had to be taken care of, the basement filled with wood, cobs and coal for the winter. Corn had to be picked from the field. Ed, my brother, and I had our team of horses and my Dad and sister Johanna had their team, and we got all the corn husked by hand, and filled the cribs. PLUS WE HAD TO GET READY FOR A BRIDAL SHOWER, AND THEN A WEDDING!!

A young Alphonse changing a tire.

84

February 21,1952, Dad shoveling out the car from the garage.

CHAPTER TWENTY FIVE
The Wedding

· ·

October 29, 1946, was coming so fast- My Wedding Day- I was practicing writing my new name, Mrs. Alphonse Mages.

One sunny day my Mother, and my sisters drove to Mankato, Minnesota. About eighty miles away to the, "Lorraine Bridal Shop," where my sister Lydia had also gotten her wedding dress about four years earlier. What a disappointment to find that they had only two dresses in my size. One had short sleeves, one had long sleeves. Dresses were not ordered, so I had to choose a dress in the correct size. We tried Brett's Department Store also, but no luck there. I did get the dress with the long sleeves. It was a lovely dress. A shimmery soft material with a long train. We were still finding that things were hard to get after the war. Factories haven't caught up with the demand. Mother tried to buy sheets and towels, and couldn't get those either. But anyway, Martha and Adella, my sisters, were able to get bridesmaid dresses. Identical ones. One was pink and one was yellow. Alphonse's sister, Diane, was going to be the flower girl Martha had a blue bridesmaid dress from a different wedding, and we gave it to Alphonse, so his Mother could make a dress for five year old Diane from that dress.

The guys also had a hard time getting suits. Alphonse said they only had one suit in his size, but he looked great in it. Alphonse's brother, Albin and my brother, Ed were the best men. Those days you did not order dresses. You bought what was available. You did not rent a tux, that service was not available.

You did not schedule your wedding with the priest a year before the wedding. You did not have meetings with the priest, only about fifteen minutes the night before the wedding at wedding practice.

The reception would be at the Kodet home, so we limited the guest list to about seventy people. Alphonse had many aunts and uncles, and so did I. More than we had room for.

We would have three tables' settings about twelve places apiece. One in the dining room, one in the living room, and one in the downstairs bedroom. Mother and Dad would store their bed in the garage that day. We would borrow a big table from Joe and Louise Kodet, and get folding chairs at the church. Mother got new tablecloths, china, goblets, glasses, silverware for the brides table in the living room, and those would be given to the wedding couple later. There would be two settings. Those waiting for the second setting would sit in the front porch, and the men could go out, and play horseshoe. For the dinner I asked six of my friends to be waitresses, and I made fancy aprons for all of them.

Dad always had a keg of beer available. Mother had two cooks hired to help with the food. Mrs. Rose Moudry helped out at many weddings. Ruth Cornwell was a neighbor lady who also helped. They came the day before, and made all the kolachy, a Czechoslovakian sweet roll, and the dinner rolls, and roasted the meat. Alphonse's parents had sent over about six geese ready to be roasted. My Dad also smoked ham earlier, so that was prepared also. They peeled lots of potatoes, and got everything ready to go. Ruth went home that night, but Mrs. Moudry stayed all night. All the tables had to be set in the morning.

Martha, Adella and I had gone to town to have our hair done, as the wedding Mass was at 9 am the next morning. Only the bride and groom would receive Holy Communion, so I had to be careful not to eat or drink after midnight. We put a towel over the water pail in the pantry, so I wouldn't accidentally take a drink. At that time fasting started at midnight.

Albin had come home from the army about three weeks
before the wedding. Ed had been home in time to help with corn
picking, so those two were the best men. Rehearsal was the
night before the wedding, so Alphonse's family all came, and we
all went to St. Mary's in Bechyn. Rehearsal went well. Alphonse
and I both went to confession, and then we had a meeting with
the priest for about fifteen minutes. Father C. Zwicky was our
priest. We went back to our farm, and decorated the car. We
girls had already put up decorations at the house. We had lunch,
and were ready for the next day.

A light rain was falling. The weather was warm though.
October had been a beautiful month. Alphonse and Albin
came with his car, and then the rest of the Mages family came.
Alphonse looked so handsome in his new suit. I was dressed in
my gown and veil, and so were my sisters in their bridesmaid
dresses. My Mother and Dad were in their fine clothes, and my
family was all set to go to my wedding.

Alphonse gave me a three strand pearl necklace to wear, and I
picked up my bouquet of big chrysanthemums. The Mothers had
corsages, and Martha and Adella carried mums. The men all had
mum boutonnieres.

The rain had stopped, still cloudy, but looking good. I rode
to church with Dad and Mom, and I'm sure I was nervous as
Dad walked me down the aisle, but there was my groom waiting
for me. The choir was doing a wonderful job without me or my
sisters.

We said our vows with our families all looking on, and our
rings were blessed. Alphonse put my ring on my finger, and
I gave him a ring also. We received Holy Communion, as we
started our new life. The choir sang, "On This Day O Beautiful
Mother," as our last hymn.

We came out of the church, and Alphonse kissed me, our
first kiss in our marriage. The sun was shining as everyone
congratulated us. What a wonderful Day!!!!!!!!!!!!!!!

We drove to the farm, and started to go to the house. The cooks blocked the door. They each held on to an end of a dish towel, and said," We had to pay to get in." That was a custom I had forgotten about. Alphonse gave them ten dollars, and they escorted us to a small table set up for our breakfast, as we had received Holy Communion, and we were the only ones that had not eaten breakfast. So while everyone else was visiting we had breakfast.

The day went so fast. A delicious meal at noon, and then the wedding party had to go to Redwood Falls to the studio to have our wedding pictures taken, but my brother, Junior, had taken my shoe, and didn't know where it had ended up. It was found, and we were on our way. When we returned we opened our wedding gifts. Then there was supper, and many of the guests left to get ready for the dance. Most farmers had chores to do. The horseshoe games were kept busy most of the day, also cards were played.

October 29,1946, The wedding party, L-R: Ed Kodet, Albin Mages, Alphonse, Barbara, Diane, Adella and Martha

The dance was held in the Morton, Minnesota City Hall, as it was more convenient to both sides of the family. The, "Red Raven Band," played the old time music. We had met at a dance right here in Morton, so it was full circle for us. Alphonse and I were dancing our wedding dance.

During the dance Martha was told that Clarence Serbus, her fiancé, was coming home that night on the bus, so she went with some friends to meet the bus. How wonderful to see him again, home from the Army, home from Japan.

Another wedding coming up, about two and half months later on January 14, 1947 Martha married Clarence Serbus.

CHAPTER TWENTY SIX
Our First Home

· ·

We knew where we were going to live, on the Jens Miller farm, but Jens was very slow about moving out. The auction he was going to have in September didn't happen until the middle of November. We were finally going to take over the house, but first it had to be cleaned.

We were staying at the Mages house in the meantime. I learned to do cooking in the Mages style, dandelion salad, fried green and red tomatoes, so that was a plus. My Mother, and my brother, Ed, came to help clean our house one beautiful November day. Oswald, Elizabeth, Alphonse's parents, Albin, Alphonse's brother, and Alphonse and I were armed with soap, buckets, brooms and mops. Ed, Albin and Alphonse found an old Sears Catalog, and had a fun time looking through that. They had a fire going outside to burn garbage. The door between the kitchen, and dining room was the backboard for Jen's coal pail. He chewed tobacco, and that door had so much spit on it, that it went into the fire. The dining room had a built in corner cupboard, that was nice. The kitchen cupboards looked good. We bought a wood stove heater from my brother, Emil, so that was our heat while we worked. No stove in the kitchen. Jens had a two burner gas deal covered with grease, so that went out the door. BUT WE HAD ELECTRICITY!!!!!!!! I teased Alphonse that I married him because then I would have electricity, Just like I teased him that if the windows were open after we went to bed, and it started to rain, if he got up instead of me having to, then I would marry him.

Alphonse had bought the pump jack motor at the auction, so we went to get a pail of water, we just flipped the switch. No more using the pump handle. There was no running water in the house, so the biffy was out by the shed. The weeds by the shed were as high as the roof, and the cattle yard fence was going to have to be totally replaced.

Over the next few weeks we put up wall paper, and did some painting. We moved in between Christmas and New Years. Our wedding and shower gifts were put in use. We had a party for our friends on New Year's Eve. Our first party.

My Mother and Dad had ordered two stoves, one for us, and one for Martha, my sister who was getting married two months after us, a combination gas range. That also was in demand after the war, so we had to wait for it to come. We were using an old fashioned wood stove range with the warming ovens above, and the water reservoir on the side. Just like at home. That worked pretty well, and kept the kitchen warm.

But I had an electric Maytag washing machine, and an electric iron. We still had no telephone, but there was talk of a party line coming.

The barn was gotten ready for cows and pigs. Alphonse had bought the cow tank at the auction, so the cows had a place to drink. Alphonse received six cows from his Dad, and I received two cows, and a yearling heifer, so we had to do milking by hand again. Little by little we got our farm going.

We had ordered 300 chickens that spring, and put them in the brooder house. Alphonse

Alphonse feeding the chickens

worked up the garden plot that spring, and together we planted seeds. There were three apple trees, and a plum orchard in back.

We used machinery with his Dad, but the corn planter had to be used with horses, so Alphonse planted corn with horses that spring. Oswald had bought an F-20 tractor. It had a cultivator that was attached. The small grain was put in with a seeder that spread seed on top of the ground, then had to be disked into the soil.

There was an old fashioned single corn crib sitting practically in the middle of the yard between the house and barn. One day the cows got out, and saw the corn in the crib. So I went to chase them back in the yard. I took my broom along, and ended up breaking my broom on one stubborn cow. I never heard the end of that one.

It didn't take long before Alphonse hooked up the tractor to that crib, and put it in a more favorable spot.

We had a circle drive that went around three big shade trees, and in the spring the roses on the south side of the house were blooming.

And we had a dog!!!! He was a medium size black collie looking dog. When Jens moved, he couldn't take his dog along, so we had a faithful friend. Bobby was his name. God had blessed us.

Alphonse mowing our lawn.

I am sorry, my dear family, that now that I'm married, that is the end of my, "Kodet Days on the Farm."

I am now married to a Mages, and anything I write in the hereafter will be a Mages Memory.

Our first home

Our first cattle

CHAPTER TWENTY SEVEN
Bechyn Now 2015

· ·

Bechyn still has a gravel road going through this little settlement. The paved road is a mile to the west connecting the towns of Redwood Falls and Danube, Minnesota. They used to say that if you blinked your eyes when driving through Bechyn you could miss the town.

The long line of elm trees that used to shade the parked cars is all gone, victims of the Dutch Elm disease many years ago. My Grandpa and Grandma Kojetin's house is still there. The couple that bought it added on to the east side, and raised a young family there.

They are adults now. The parish of St. Mary's house was sold to a family, and their children have grown, and gone out into the world.

The church stands surrounded by green lawns, and flower beds, so lovely with it's tall steeple reaching to the sky. It is closed now, except for a funeral or possible a wedding, but always open on Czech Day when the whole town comes alive with thousands of people coming back to

The left building is now the Henryville Township Hall, and the building on the right use to be, "Charleys."

95

celebrate their Czech heritage. There is always music in the air.

The lawn behind the church is kept weedless, and mowed. Many trees were planted there years ago, and they provide shade for all the activities. There is room for two big tents, and many picnic tables.

The cemetery is next to the church. There are the graves of my Dad and Mom, and my brothers, Emil and Ed and sister, Johanna. My Dad lived to be 92 years old. My Mother died of kidney cancer that turned into spinal cancer, and then brain cancer in 1981, she was 81 years old as she was born in 4-13-1900. Emil died in 1993 after a stroke when he was 74 years old, and Ed died in 1959 at the age of 35 years old of a heart attack while driving his car home from town. Johanna died in 2010 after a stroke. She had her 90th birthday party just six weeks before her death. Their graves are nearby. My sister, Lydia and her husband, Joe Serbus, were both killed in a car accident on Easter Monday, April 4, 1994. It was a freak snowstorm, and caused icy roads. Lydia was 72 years old, and Joe was 78 years old. They are buried in St. Patrick's Catholic Cemetery at Birch Coulie near Franklin, Minnesota. There are graves of our two babies, Alphonse's and mine, Robert was born prematurely and weighed 3 pounds 14 ounces, and was a twin to Richard. His lungs weren't developed fully, and he passed away on his second day of life, December 06, 1953. Mary Beth was 6 weeks old when God called her home. She died of lumbar pneumonia on March 04, 1959. Our two little angels in heaven. My Great Grandparents, Wencel and Anna Kojetin are buried there. My Great Grandfather, helped establish, and build the first church, St. Mary's, in Bechyn, and named the town after their homeland, Bechyne, Czechoslovakia. Nine of us, Alphonse's and my children, Dan and wife Arlene, Larry and wife Maggie, Debbie and husband Larry Fischer, Curt, Linda and Myself, were privileged to visit Bechyne, Czechoslovakia in September, 2012. Great Grandma, Anna, passed away in the influenza epidemic in 1918.

Wencel and Mary Kodet my paternal Grandparents, and Wencel and Mary Kojetin, my maternal Grandparents are buried there. The two names Wencel and Mary were very common. The name Wencel Kojetin went down to the fourth generation. I have many Aunts, Uncles and cousins buried there. The cemetery is kept up with perpetual care. A few years ago, a strong windstorm took down some of the tall pine trees that were originally planted there. There are still a few left, and they stand tall reaching to the sky.

It is the first week of May, 2015. My sister, Mary Lou Butzer, and I walk through the cemetery. We had brought flowers along with us to place on the graves, but the wind was so strong, we thought we would wait until later before Memorial Day to place them. It is a sad day as we also remember our husbands that have passed away. May they rest in peace.

We see the area of green grass that used to be the baseball field. It is now used as a parking lot on Czech Day. The big cottonwoods that used to stand on the edge of the west lawn are gone. They used to shade the bazaar area years ago, the bingo stand, children's games, baked goods, country store, fancy work and more.

The house where Archie Wertish lived is gone, but his shed that sheltered his road grader is still standing. Maybe the road grader is still stored there. We drove, "uptown," where the two stores had been. They are both closed, and have been for a long time. "Charley's," has been turned into a garage with two double doors. It stands beside the Bechyn Hall. That building used to be the first church. It was pulled into its location, and fixed up as the Bechyn Hall. There were many meetings, bridal showers and dances held there. Music was played by the Kodet Brother's, my Dad and his brothers, Joe and Adolph, or the Kohout Family Band or Roger Kodet and the Cards Band, also the Kassel Band. It has been well taken care of. It has vinyl siding, a steel roof, and a sign on the front names it as the Henryville Township Hall. It still has the four low windows in the front. I remember when the windows would be open for summer dances, no screens. Ralph Scharfencamp, Alphonse's best friend from Morgan, Minnesota, was sitting on the window sill, and someone pushed

him right out the window. He didn't get hurt as he didn't fall too far. He later married a Bechyn girl, Angie Malecek, who were our lifelong friends, and our daughter, Lisa's Godparents. Dances were held every Sunday night, and there was always a crowd.

The first church, later the Bechyn Hall and now the Henryville Township Hall.

Across the road was the store called," George's." It is closed, but the upstairs apartment had been used for a long time. There are a couple of houses close by that are still being used.

There was never a school in Bechyn, but one half mile away in the country to the south was a country school, District #27. That was known as the Bechyn School. The school has been closed for many years, and most school children went to Redwood Falls or Danube Schools.

As Mary Lou and I left Bechyn, we were surrounded by fertile land that had been planted to corn or beans. We spotted a field where the corn was just peeking through the soil. It was a sign of hope for the future.

A couple of years ago I traveled with family members to Europe, where we toured Northern Italy, Austria, Germany and the Czech Republic. One of our main destinations was Bechyne, Czechoslovakia located in, and "Bohemia," in the Czech Republic. It lies in the midst of fertile farmland, and is now a thriving community of six thousand people. We were in awe as we crossed the bridge on the Ludnice River, and saw the town nestled in the valley with the castle up on the hill. HOW

BEAUTIFUL!!!! Our bus driver took us right to the Square where we took pictures by the big fountain. St. Matthew's church was opposite the side of the little shoppes.

How wonderful it was to walk in the footsteps of Grandma Mary Kojetin, who came to this country when she was sixteen, Grandpa Wencel and Grandma Mary Kodet, and our other ancestors that had arrived earlier. It was a memory I hold close to my heart. We moved on to the other Catholic church in Bechyne, a couple of blocks from the Square, St. Michael's. We explored the cemetery there that had many familiar names. We said some prayers for the people buried there. We found graves with the names Kodet and Swovoda, but no names of Kojetin.

How fitting it is that we should travel back to Bechyn, Minnesota, and remember the traditions of our little town, and St. Mary's Catholic Church. That we too can walk in the footsteps of our parents, grandparents, and great grandparents.

Oh Lord!! Thank you for all your blessings.

PHOTO GALLERY

1924, Emil, Lydia, Johanna, Baby Ed

1924, Johanna, Baby Ed, Emil and Lydia

1929, Emil, Johanna, Dad, Lydia, Ed, Martha

1924, Emil and Johanna

1929, Dad and Stanley Malecek

1937, L-R: Junior, Ed, Dad, Emil and Harold Benesh. The threshing machine by the old house

09,1929, Dad and Baby Barbara

09, 1929, Martha, Johanna, Emil, Baby Barbara, Lydia and Ed

09,19,1929, Mother and Baby Barbara

09,1929, Martha, Johanna, Baby Barbara, Emil, Lydia behind Ed

1932, Dad with his daughters holding Baby Adella, Barbara, Martha, Johanna and Lydia

1932, Three year old Barbara
making mud pies.

1930,Martha, Ed, Lydia,
Johanna, Emil and Mother

1932, Ed, 8 years old, Martha, 6 years old,
and Barbara, 3 years old.

Early 1930's Mother and Dad

June 25, 1933, Johanna and Emil
making their Solemn Communion

1934, Ed and Lydia making
their Solemn Communion

July 12, 1933, Emil, Johanna and Lydia

1940, Mother and her sister,
Emma Halliday

September, 1936, Emil

1936, Martha

July 13, 1938, Lydia

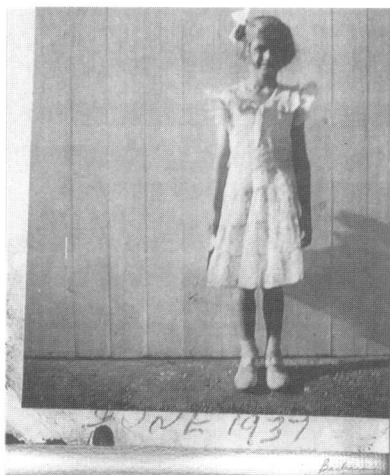

June, 1937, Barbara,
Eight years old

September, 1936, Johanna

July 02,1939, Adella eight years old.

December, 1938, Mary Lou and Adellal

1937, Ed standing in front
of the south side of the house
where the porch is.

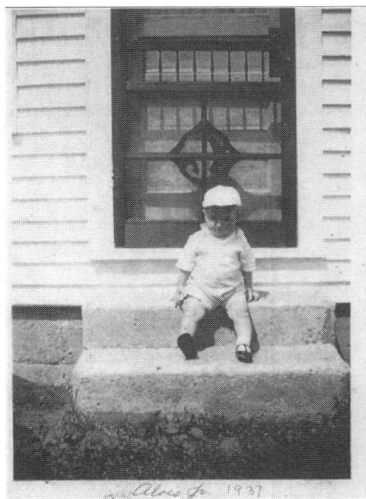

1937, Alois Jr, Aka: Junior.

1941, Junior.

August, 1944, Mary Lou

April 15, 1945, Barbara and Adella

1944, Dad and Mom married 26 years.

April 28,1946, Barbara

1946, Junior's First Communion

May13, 1945, Martha, Ed and Barbara.

September 29,1947, Mother and Ed

May, 1945, Emil, Ed, Junior and Dad.

October 21, 1945, Martha, Note Junior in the background on Tom, the horse's back.

109

1945, Ed and Junior

February 27, 1947, Junior and Ed.

February,1946, Barbara

February 09,1946,
Martha and Barbara

May 29, 1933, Barbara with her birthday cake.

1947, Adella and Junior

January 09,1946, Adella, Junior and Barbara. It was 20 degrees below zero that day.

1946, Dad and Mom

September, 1946, Martha, Mary Lou, Mom, Adella and Johanna.

February 07,1946, Barbara, Martha, Mary Lou and Junior

January 14, 1947, Wedding of
Clarence Serbus and Martha Kodet.

November 10, 1948, wedding of
Jean Hensley and Ed Kodet, Albin and
Adella Mages were attendants.

April 13, 1948, wedding of Adella Kodet
and Albin Mages

1947, Mary Lou with Junior
on the ladder.

May 15, 1949, Mother on
our front steps

May 15, 1949, Dad and Mom.

May 22, 1949, Adella and Junior.

June, 1950, Emil and his family, Dick,
JoAnn, Diane, Emil and, "Babe," (Rosella.)

114

1950, Lydia and Joe Serbus family, Barbara, Lydia holding, Claire, Joe, Judy and Jean.

May 10, 1953, Junior driving the first car, Dad standing behind

May, 1953, Dad and Junior.

August, 1952, Dad, Mom and Junior.

July 28, 1954, wedding of Mary Lou Kodet and Jim Butzer.

May 30, 1954, Junior graduated from high school.

115

April, 1946, Junior and Alphonse's brother, Clarence Mages.

July 28, 1954, Mary Lou's wedding day with all her sisters, Barbara, Adella, Mary Lou, Johanna, Lydia and Martha.

Spring, 1957, Junior on the tractor.

1965, after St. Patrick's Day Blizzard. Dad and Mother's retirement home in Olivia,Minnesota. Adella's daughter, Carol, and her husband bought the house, and live there now.

October, 1958, Dad and Mother's 40th wedding anniversary.

Kodets celebrate 60

Mr. and Mrs. A.E. Kodet of Olivia were guests of honor Sunday, Oct. 22, at a dinner party as they celebrated their 60th wedding anniversary. Among the 150 guests were their children, grandchildren, and great-grandchildren.

The party was held at St. Aloysius Church Hall, and the decorated anniversary cake was made and decorated by a granddaughter, Mrs. Richard Welshons of Fridley.

A.E. Kodet and Barbara Kojetin were married at St. Mary's Catholic Church in Bechyn on Oct. 29, 1918. They farmed near Bechyn until they retired and moved to Olivia.

They had nine children: Edward, deceased; Emil of Litchfield, Mrs. Jim Butzer (Mary Lou) of Eagan, Mrs. Alphonse Mages (Barbara) of Sleepy Eye, Mrs. Albin Mages (Adella) and Johanna Kodet of Olivia, Alois, Jr. of North Redwood, Mrs. Joseph L. Serbus (Lydia) and Mrs. Clarence Serbus (Martha), of rural Bird Island. They were all able to be present for the day.

10-1978

MR. AND MRS. ALOIS KODET SR.

Alois E. Kodet- February 12, 1892- 1984
Barbara Kojetin Kodet- April 13, 1900- 1981, Married October 29, 1918
Wencel Kojetin-1866-1940
Mary Horesji Kojetin-1870-1970, Married May 18, 1891
Wencel Kodet - died April 01,1927
Mary Swoboda Kodet-April 01,1861-May, 1935, Married June 25, 1883

The Kojetin grave stones at the St.
Mary's Cemetery in Bechyn. The older
stones are craved in their native language of
Czechoslovakian That stone
belongs to Wencel Kojetin II and
Anna Swoboda Kojetin.

Wencel Kojetin III and Mary
Horesji Kojetin

Wencel Kodet II and Mary
Swoboda Kodet

Alois E. Kodet and Barbara
Kojetin Kodet

August 29, 2012, entering Bechyne, Czechoslovakia

The town square in Bechyne, Czechoslovakia,
L-R: Debbie Fischer, Linda Gall, Maggie and Larry
Mages, Mom (Barbara Kodet Mages,) and Arlene
Mages, August 29, 2012.

119

BARBARA KODET MAGES

Larry and Maggie Mages in Bechyne, Czechoslovakia at the fountain in the town square. August 29,2012

Barbara Kodet Mages with daughter Linda Gall at St. Michael's cemetery in Bechyne, Czechoslovakia where we found Kodet and Swoboda graves. August 29,2012

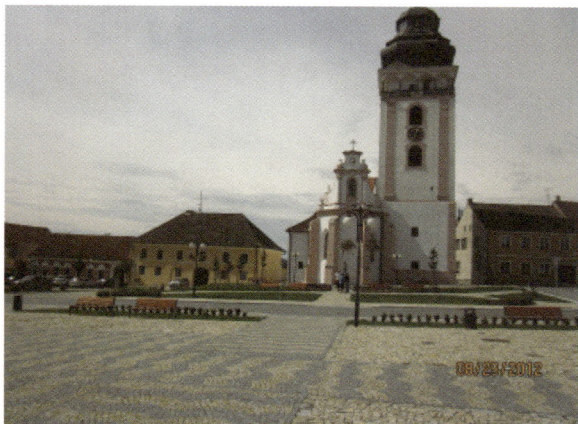

August 29,2012, Bechyne, Czechoslovakia, the town square. St. Matthew's Catholic Church in the middle.

Larry pretending to hear confession of our German cousin, Tobi Mages whose family traveled with us in Europe. This confessional is at St. Barbara's Chapel in Bechyne, Czechoslovakia

August 29,2012, At an outdoor restaurant in Bechyne, Czechoslovakia with our German cousins. L-R: Linda Gall, Larry Fischer, Helmut Mages, Larry Mages, Dan Mages, Arlene Mages, Maggie Mages, Barbara Kodet Mages, Curt Mages, Tobi Mages and Birgit Mages. Debbie Mages Fischer is behind the camera taking this picture.

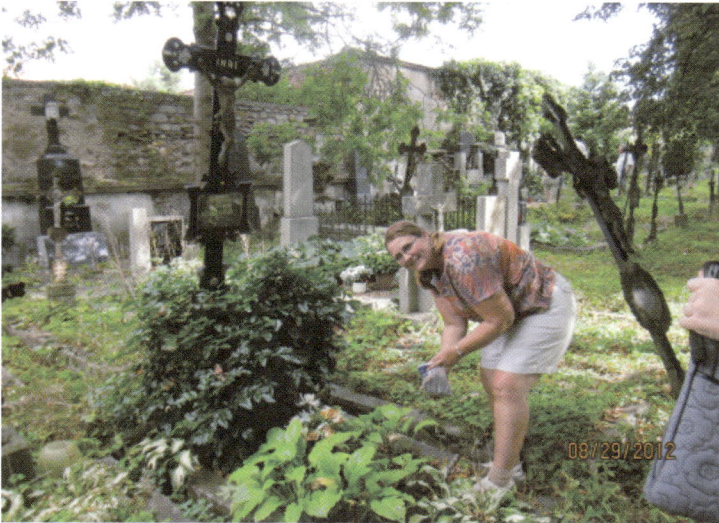

Debbie Fischer doing some maintenance at a
Kodet grave site at St. Michael's church in Bechyne, Czechoslovakia

Kodet grave sites at St. Michael's cemetery in Bechyne, Czechoslovakia. We
were told that ova at the end of a name means a woman is buried there.

St. Michael's Catholic Church cemetery in Bechyne, Czechoslovakia The grave site is a Swoboda.

Photo on the left is in front of St. Michael's Catholic Church in Bechyne, Czechoslovakia. We were in Europe for sixteen days, and we walked between six and ten miles a day, so on these days it was nice for me at eighty three years of age to use a wheel chair that my children, and our German cousins, so graciously pushed me in. L-R: Larry Fischer, Linda Gall, Larry Mages, Curt Mages, Barbara Kodet Mages, Debbie Fischer, Maggie Mages, Arlene Mages and Dan Mages.

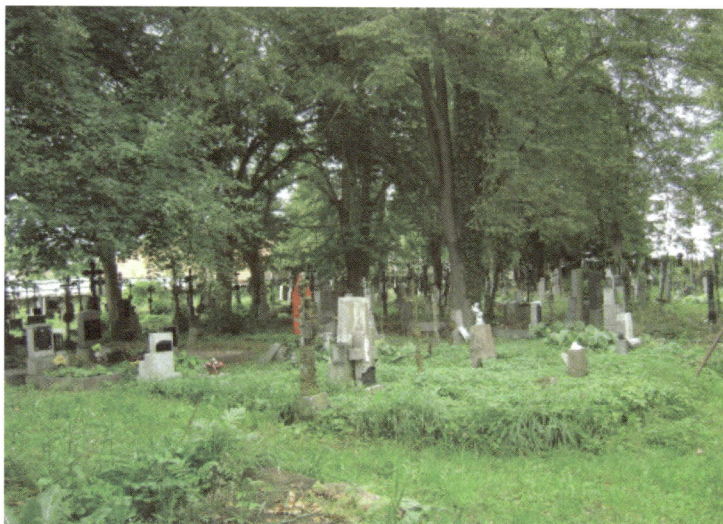

You can see by this picture that the cemetery of our ancestors at St. Michael's is neglected. It was sad to all of us to see that, but when we found our ancestors grave sites we were so amazed. We all said a prayer for all those dear to us in the wonderful town of Bechyne, Czechoslovakia.

L-R:, Barbara Plath, Linda Gall, Lisa Schmitz, Betty Jass, Alphonse, Barbara , Nancy Strate, Debbie Fischer, Donna Nelson, Back row, Tom, Mike, Curt, Jeff, Dan, Duane, Larry, John and Rick.